The Positiv(Handbook

Drawing on Judy Hutchings many years of work with parents and children, *The Positive Parenting Handbook* is a concise, straightforward guide that offers simple solutions to daily dilemmas. The clear and easy advice provides parents with skills and tools that support positive parent/child relationships for happy and confident children. It explains common behaviour problems in young children and offers expert advice on:

- How to build strong bonds and let children know they are important to you
- How to encourage behaviour we want to see through praise and small rewards
- Giving instructions that children are more likely to follow
- How ignoring some unwanted behaviours can be helpful
- Strategies for managing difficult behaviour
- Teaching new behaviour to our children
- Developing children's language.

It includes six case studies of how these strategies have helped real families with everyday problems at bedtime and mealtimes, during toilet training, out shopping and when children experience anxiety.

Together with suggestions of other useful books and information sources, *The Positive Parenting Handbook* is ideal for all parents, including those of children with diagnosed developmental difficulties, and the range of professionals who work with them.

Professor Judy Hutchings was an NHS Clinical Child Psychologist for 37 years, and since 1988 has also worked as a researcher at Bangor University, where she set up the Centre for Evidence Based Early Intervention. She introduced parenting programmes into treatment and preventive services and undertakes research trials on services for children with behavioural problems, including developing the EPaS (Enhancing Parenting Skills) programme. In 2011, she was awarded an OBE for her work with children and families.

The Positive Parenting Handbook

Developing Happy and Confident Children

Judy Hutchings

Routledge
Taylor & Francis Group

LONDON AND NEW YORK

First published 2020
by Routledge
2 Park Square, Milton Park, Abingdon, Oxon OX14 4RN

and by Routledge
52 Vanderbilt Avenue, New York, NY 10017

Routledge is an imprint of the Taylor & Francis Group, an informa business

© 2020 Judy Hutchings

British Library Cataloguing-in-Publication Data
A catalogue record for this book is available from the British Library

Library of Congress Cataloging-in-Publication Data
A catalog record has been requested for this book

ISBN: 978-0-367-23380-8 (hbk)
ISBN: 978-0-367-23381-5 (pbk)
ISBN: 978-0-429-27960-7 (ebk)

Typeset in Stempel Garamond
by Swales & Willis, Exeter, Devon, UK

Contents

Foreword by Judy Hutchings

This little book introduces some important parenting skills or tools that support positive parent-child relationships. Many of them are common sense and are what most parents do most of the time without realising it. But for parents with children that have particular challenges, these ideas have been used in many programmes to support them and help their children. Chapter 1 gives a brief summary of typical behaviour problems. Chapter 2 looks at how to build a strong relationship with our children. Chapter 3 describes how to encourage behaviour we want to see more of in our children through praise and small rewards. Chapter 4 describes ways of giving instructions that will make it more likely that children will follow them. Chapter 5 explains how ignoring some unwanted behaviours can be helpful. Chapter 6 describes some constructive ways of managing problem behaviour. Chapter 7 focuses on skills for teaching new behaviour and Chapter 8 emphasises the importance of developing children's language skills. The first version of this book was written over 25 years ago as help sheets for parents of children with challenging behaviour, but the ideas come from many years of research that tell us what parents can do to support good parent-child relationships that result in happy and confident children.

The ideas are helpful to any parent, including those of children with diagnosed developmental difficulties, who can also have challenging behaviour and/or other difficulties that are not a direct consequence of their condition.

With thanks to Diana Williams for working with us and providing the illustrations.

The book is dedicated to Mary Last. Mary who was head of the Child Clinical Psychology Service in North West Wales for many years and helped with the development of the parenting programme at the Gwynedd Child and Family Research Centre in the 1990s. Mary supported many children and families during her career. She died in 1998 and is still missed.

The Children's Early Intervention Trust (CEIT)

The first edition of this book was published by CEIT in 2013.

CEIT is a registered charity that was established in 2007. Working closely with the Centre for Evidence Based Early Intervention (CEBEI) in the School of Psychology, Bangor University CEIT has funded research into programmes that support children's social and emotional development through work with parents, children and teachers and disseminates findings that underpin the ideas found in the book.

www.bangor.ac.uk/psychology/cebei/

1 Introduction

Understanding common behaviour problems in young children

Children's behaviour problems, like tantrums, hitting, spitting, swearing and running away, are simple and easy to learn and are very common, particularly during children's early years. This is when they do not have sufficient language to ask for things or understand that they cannot have something at that moment. In fact a lot of the skills that we want children to learn are helped if they have sufficient language to communicate what they want and understand what we want them to do. Waiting, taking turns, sticking at something or recognising that other people want something different are hard to learn and depend, to a large extent, on children's ability to use language to understand other people and to manage their own behaviour. Importantly they can also, increasingly, use their thinking skills to manage their own behaviour when they become frustrated or are faced with problems. It is important to see the behaviour that we want from children as something that they have not yet learned.

Sometimes we try out solutions to everyday problems that don't work, often through lack of sufficient thought about why the problem behaviour is occurring. So we need to work out the reason(s) behind the behaviour and decide on realistic, achievable goals that will replace problem behaviours. To be successful we have to identify the events occurring around each problem behaviour that will help explain it. This will clarify whether the child's behaviour achieves a positive consequence, avoids an instruction, is developmentally unachievable or is avoidance of an anxiety-provoking situation.

Antecendents – when and under what circumstances does the problem occur?

The first thing to identify is the situation in which problem behaviour occurs. We call this the antecedent. A problem might only occur when one parent gives the instruction, for a particular instruction, in the presence of particular people or when the child is tired or hungry. It might only occur when there is a particular programme on the TV that the child wants to watch. So we need to identify what else is going on, was it bedtime? A meal time? Did it involve more than one child? Were there visitors? And where it was occurring – at home? In a shop? At a friend's house?

Behaviour – what does the child do?

The second step in understanding the problem is to get a really clear picture of what the child does. Do they argue, ignore, run and hide, hit someone etc.?

Consequence – what response does the child's behaviour achieve?

The final step is to identify what happens in response to the child's behaviour or the consequence. Of course it may not happen every time, sometimes we say no and stick to it, whereas at other times we might give in for the sake of peace and quiet.

This process of describing problem situations in terms of Antecendents, Behaviour and Consequences, is generally known as the ABC approach and is really helpful in working out why children behave the way they do and deciding what are realistic alternatives. This ABC process is key to deciding how to deal with problem behaviours.

Functions of child behaviour – general principles

Your child may have tantrums or present challenges for lots of different reasons. The same problem behaviour can serve different functions, sometimes it can be a way of avoiding an instruction, such as to go to bed; at other times it can be a way of getting a demand met, such as for sweets or a drink; and on another occasion it can be a way of dealing with frustration and generating help when things go wrong. A problem behaviour may get attention, but it might also occur because the child cannot avoid the problem because the alternative is developmentally beyond them or may not have been learned. This is why it is important to look at each situation where problems occur, because each different situation may need to be dealt with in different ways.

The same behaviour problem occurs for different reasons in different children. One child's refusal to go to school might be because they are being teased and have become anxious about school, another child might find being at home more rewarding than school, because they can play computer games all day; another child can get rewarded by meeting other truanting friends and engaging in risky activities, such as drinking or smoking.

What follows are examples of common reasons for the occurrence of problems:

i) Attention

One of the most frequently heard explanations for problem behaviour is that it is for attention. Young children need lots of attention and if they cannot get it in positive ways they can find other ways to get it, because at one level "any attention is better than none". Getting attention for problem behaviour is a risky strategy, since parents often respond inconsistently and children and adults can be alternately rewarded. The parental attention that rewards the behaviour may not be particularly pleasant, but, for a young child who gets insufficient positive attention, it may suffice in the short term even if it does not work every time. This is why giving positive attention (see Chapter 2) and investing our time in our children for their own sakes is so important. If children get enough positive attention they will not need to use problem behaviour to get it. Since we also tend to do things for people we like, investing in our relationship with our children can also make them much more willing to follow instructions.

ii) The problem behaviour may achieve a tangible reward

Although parental attention may have established problem behaviours, over time it may cease to be reinforcing, particularly if parents become more negative and critical in trying to control their child's behaviour. So, children are likely to use problematic behaviour to achieve short-term tangible rewards instead. Parents may "give in" to stop the confrontation, such as giving a child a biscuit or sweets at the supermarket till because the child has learned to persist with an aggressive behaviour and cease only when the demand for the sweets or biscuits is met. In another situation the problem behaviour may be a threat that achieves a reward, for example, saying to another child "give me that toy or I will hit you".

iii) The child's demand is immediately complied with by the parent

Sometimes the child does not "need" to have a tantrum because the parent has learned to comply with the child's demands immediately, so avoiding a tantrum. Identifying this pattern of reward is harder, because the parent has learned to pre-empt problem child behaviour by meeting the demand before the child has a tantrum. A 13-year-old child with a significant developmental difficulty demanded that cola and crisps were on the table when he arrived home from school in a taxi. His past, very aggressive tantrums had led his mother to avoid any confrontation by providing what he wanted *before* he asked for it. Teaching him to greet his mum and wait for his cola and crisps using the principles described in this book, took some time.

iv) Avoiding or resisting following an instruction
Refusal to follow instructions is typical of children both with and without behavioural problems. Most children follow more than 50% of instructions, and we generally accept that, but some children follow less than others and need more support to learn to do this. There are a number of reasons why children fail to follow instructions:

a) The child may be capable of following the instruction but may not have been taught what to do.

b) The child may not be able to do what is being asked because the instruction is not developmentally appropriate.

c) It could be because what the child is doing at the time – playing with Lego, watching TV, etc. – is more rewarding than what they are being asked to do, such as getting ready for bed.

d) Sometimes the task is developmentally appropriate, but not explained clearly enough. This is a particular challenge for children whose language skills may not be sufficient to correctly interpret what is required of them. Chapter 4 has some key ideas for helping children to follow instructions.

v) The child's behaviour generates support.

Some problem behaviours generate help to deal with frustration

Sometimes children are frustrated by their failure at an activity and a tantrum is a call for help. The child may be doing a puzzle, building a tower or trying to get dressed and it goes wrong. This can often be a problem for inattentive children, such as those with ADHD (who tend to rush at tasks) or those with developmental challenges (who may have communication difficulties).

vi) The behaviour stops something nasty from happening

Aggressive responses to a perceived or actual threat can remove the threat – for example when a child behaves aggressively towards someone who has been unkind to them in response to teasing or being excluded.

vii) The behaviour avoids a stressful situation

Some behaviours reduce stress through avoidance of what appear to be problem situations. This can occur in situations that generate anxiety, such as social situations or transitions from one activity to another, for example, for children with an autistic spectrum disorder. This also applies to children with other specific difficulties, such as dyslexia, who can avoid situations that demand the skills that they find challenging. Forms of avoidance that produce severe physiological responses are described as phobias.

The ideas in this little book will suggest ways of addressing these everyday challenges that have been used to help many parents over the last 40 years.

2 Building a positive relationship

Letting children know that they are important to us

Thirty-five years ago advice to parents about how to encourage their children's good behaviour concentrated on two things. First they were advised to look for any "good" behaviour that the child showed and to notice and praise it and, by doing so, to make it more likely to happen again. Then they were told to look at "problem" behaviour and work out ways to make it less likely to happen again. Ideas about how to get better at doing both of these things are included in the chapters on rewarding good behaviour and managing difficult behaviour. However, we now know that there is something fundamental that is more important than both of these activities and must come first. That is investing time in our children, in order to learn about them and their interests and to let them know that they are important to us. This chapter is about what that is and how to do it.

The things that children do that parents think of as "good" or "bad" only account for a small amount of their time, in fact less than one quarter of it. What children do the rest of the time can be seen by parents as "doing their own thing" or playing, in which parents sometimes take little interest. After all, it provides a welcome opportunity for a busy parent to get on with daily chores. Parents

who have a difficult or demanding child, or a child with learning difficulties or other special needs, inevitably have to spend more time helping their child, so the tendency to let the child "get on with it" when they are occupied may be even stronger.

Play, however, is very important to children. Showing interest in their child's play is also a way that parents can improve their relationship with their children quickly and effectively. By play we are talking about playing with toys, acting and most other things that children do without instructions from adults or that parents might like them to do on their own. When a parent shows that what their child is doing is also important to them it improves their relationship with their child and increases the likelihood that it will happen again. This spending time and taking notice of children is sometimes called "attending".

Attending lets children know that we are watching them and interested in them when they are doing something that they have chosen to do. It is not about keeping track of children's behaviour to make sure that they are behaving appropriately, which is another important skill that parents need. It is about showing interest in children for their own sake.

Parents of children with developmental challenges or difficult behaviour can spend a lot of time helping their children learn to do things that are difficult for them or trying to stop them from misbehaving or harming themselves. When children are playing or occupying themselves quietly it is easy to leave them to their own devices. But this is just when it helps to "attend" to children and to what they are doing.

Attending helps children know that their parents value them as individuals, appreciate the things that they do and are not only concerned with getting them to do as they are told. Children who are good at following instructions or advice generally do this because they have a positive relationship with their parents and want to please them because of the interest that their parents have shown in them.

Attending is a way that parents can "tune in" to the things that children are doing and notice and respond to what they are saying and doing to communicate with their parents. It also helps parents to learn more about their children, and what they can do, so as to have realistic expectations about their behaviour. When someone really listens to you and notices what you are doing it makes you feel good because you feel valued. Think of the people who care about you. You know it because they show an interest in you and let you know that your views matter to them. When a relationship between a parent and child is going well this happens naturally. Children notice their parents' attention and, in return, respond positively to it.

There is a lot that parents can do to get better at "attending". Often parents were good at attending to their babies before they could talk but found it harder to do when children got older, more mobile and more challenging; after all we have to redirect our toddlers every four minutes to keep them safe. Look at this example of a mother with her six-month-old daughter who is sitting in a high chair banging a wooden spoon on a pan lid whilst she is getting the dinner. It probably feels very familiar.

(Baby bangs)

Mother "Ooh, that's a lovely noise"

(Baby looks up at mother and bangs again with a smile)

Mother "Bang, bang, what a noise"

(Baby bangs again knocking the pan lid down)

Mother "Oh-oh, now you've knocked it down"

(Baby looks at her)

Mother "Mummy get it for you, here you are"

This mother is telling her baby what she is seeing and she describes it positively: "that's a lovely noise". She picks up her baby's attempt to communicate with her by looking at her and responds by doing what she thinks that her baby wants her to do. She does not ask questions or tell her baby what to do or how to bang.

Unfortunately, this pattern of attending often changes once children start to talk and parents can spend more time as teachers or instructors, but there are times, like when children are playing, when the job of parents is to let children know that they are watching and interested in them and what they are doing for its own sake. At these times parents need to attend to, support and encourage children in their chosen activity. Parents are their children's first, and most important, teachers and attending is a great opportunity to model an important relationship skill. Children learn as much from how we behave towards them as they do from what we ask them to do. So, remember the rule: "We are models for our children's behaviour." This is a theme that will recur throughout this book. In relation to attending, there are twenty useful rules to practice and remember.

1. **Follow your child's lead.**
   When attending to your child you must give no instructions or directions. Of course you have to take action if your child does something that he/she is not allowed to do, such as ignoring an agreed house rule (see Chapter 4 on how to get better at giving instructions and Chapter 6 on managing non-compliance and other challenging behaviours) but generally when you are attending your child is the boss.

2. **Try to avoid questions unless they clearly leave the child in charge.**
   Do not say, "Why don't you make a car?" or "What is that supposed to be?" Questions like these can

distract a child and take their concentration away from the task. Poor concentration is a problem for a growing number of children, possibly because they live in an over-stimulating world, with television being, for some children, a permanent part of their environment. An occasional question can be asked such as, "Is that going to be a shed for the horses?" but it is much better to make a comment like, "I wonder if that shed is for the horse." This leaves the child free to answer or not and they know that you are watching them closely. Another danger of questioning is that it suggests that the things the child is doing must have an end product when they may still be exploring. If you do ask a question you can answer it yourself. "What is that you are making? Oh I can see that you are still exploring using the blocks and cars."

3. **Be a reporter and describe what is happening.**

   Parents often do not know what to say when attending and the best advice is to be like the TV commentator and just describe what you see. "Now you are making a tower with the yellow bricks, and now there is a red one you are putting on top." "Now you are putting the animals into the truck and taking them on a journey."

Do not worry if your child does not appear to be paying attention to you because you are trying to unobtrusively encourage their activity. This interest can also help children to develop skills in persisting with an activity. Children really appreciate this kind of attention, although it seems unnatural to parents and they do not notice parents' awkwardness, only their interest.

4. **Use your child's name when you speak to him or her.**

Say things like: "You are putting the red block on the blue block, Peter." This also reinforces, for the child, that you are really paying attention to them. Using a child's name is also important when you are giving instructions.

5. **Make only positive comments and avoid critical comments.**

Remember this is the child's game or activity. Can you think how you have felt recently when someone has been critical of you? There is not too much right and wrong in play and, within reason, what your child chooses to play is right for them. Your job is to find something about which you can show an interest and say something positive. Removing attention from inappropriate or aggressive play is often as effective, or more effective, than giving it attention and is something that we return to in Chapter 5 on ignoring.

6. **Show your child that what they are doing is valuable by copying them.**

If your child is playing with play dough, and making

a person, you can do the same, but remember not to outshine them or to change the direction of the game. By joining in with their game you are letting your child know how important you think their game is. (Play dough is useful for encouraging children over a surprisingly wide age range to play creatively and for quite a long time and it can be made very cheaply.)

7. **Try to find a special time to attend to your child each day.**

If you are having difficulties with your child's behaviour it is likely that you are not attending often enough or that you do not do it regularly.

Whilst you are trying to help your child to improve their behaviour you should try to set aside a special time when you practice attending to your child. This is the most difficult thing to do in a busy family but some parents find time for each child just before they go to bed. Choose a time when you are not likely to be interrupted and when your child does not have something else that they want to do, like watch their favourite TV cartoon. Switch off the television and tell your child that you would like to watch them play and that they can choose what to do. The best activities are those that involve some imagination or creativity; building, modelling, drawing, pretend play with little people, animals, cars or dressing up.

If it is really difficult to engage your child you can start playing yourself with the play materials and you will probably find that they will join you. Alternatively, what a child does frequently is important to them so you may need to watch a television programme with your child and talk about it with them or watch them with their play station. By showing interest in what is important to your child you may then be able to encourage them to engage in other play activities. Television is a great educator but evidence suggests that children are watching too much and that it is having a negative impact on their concentration. See Sue Palmer's book *Toxic Childhood* for more about this, details are included in the back of this book.

8. **Listen to what your child is saying and watch them.**
   Listening to your child is more important than talking to them at this time. If you do talk you should describe what your child is doing. If your child asks what they should do you should answer but try not to tell them what to do. Whenever possible put the choice back to the child, "I wonder what you will decide to do?" It can also help to acknowledge that deciding is difficult. "It isn't easy to decide when there are so many possibilities but I think you will work it out." This allows them to problem solve and to know that you have confidence in their ability to work things out.

9. **Get your partner or a friend to watch you attending.**
   Parents of children with challenges often find attending hard – they are so used to trying to help their child or to stop them from doing something that is a problem. If you have a partner, you can watch each other and let each other know when you see them following the attending rules, or you could get a friend to sit in with you. Take turns and help each other to improve.

10. **Show your child's achievements to others.**
    Try to keep the "Lego castle" or anything the child has constructed to show to other people. Put the painting up on the wall and mention it on the phone to a relative or friend. You may also see if the child wants to keep it to work on again another day. "Shall we put the bricks back in the box or do you want to keep your model to work on tomorrow?"

11. **When you get good at attending in your special sessions start to do it at other times.**

When you feel confident that you are getting it right you can attend at other times, including when you are busy at some other task. You can attend to your child's drawing when you are peeling potatoes or to the building on the kitchen floor whilst you are loading the washing machine. Encourage your child to play where you are working. This is a lot more useful and enjoyable for your child than sitting passively in front of the television. Your child also has to learn that you cannot attend whilst you are watching your favourite TV programme or talking to a friend on the phone. It is important that you let your child know what you are going to do and that you plan what they will do while on the phone and afterwards – "You need to play quietly while I am on the phone." "When

I finish on the phone I will come and look at what you are building."

12. **Make sure that your child knows that you are attending.**

   Sit close to your child and give them your full attention. Turn your body towards them or sit opposite or beside them. One way to show that you are attending is to copy what the child does. This was particularly helpful for a deaf child for whom signing to describe what he was doing was distracting rather than helpful.

13. **Speak with enthusiasm when describing what your child is doing.**

   Although parents often say that attending makes them feel awkward, children do not usually notice

this and respond very positively to this attention. One parent reported her child saying: "Do that talking mum!" An unenthusiastic reporter would not keep their job for long. We now know from lots of research that how we say things conveys even more information than the words themselves. Think of the tone of voice and body language that helps to convey meaning when we tell someone we love them or when people describe a difficulty.

14. **Try to avoid helping your child too much.**

It is important that children have pleasure and pride in their own efforts or achievements. Either watch them or play alongside them and copy what they are doing but try to let them keep the initiative. If they ask what to do, which many children do, turn the question back by asking, "What do you think you could do?" For children who do not have a lot of self-confidence it is particularly important that they learn to make decisions in a play situation. You can hand your child materials while they are playing and support them without directing their play with a statement like: "let me know if I can get something for you or if you need anything", which does not need a reply. It is important that you only take part in the child's play if invited.

15. **You can say no to certain games when you are attending.**

Some games may not encourage creativity and, although you may not want to stop your child from playing them at other times, you may decide that there is some play to which you do not wish to attend. An example may be copying violent characters that the child might have seen on the TV. If you attend when your child plays games that you are not comfortable with they will sense this and, if your relationship with them is not good, they may pick on that sort of game every time, so withdrawing your attention is probably the best strategy. Maybe distract yourself by picking up a magazine or starting to play with a toy. Wrestling or rough physical play are not suitable for attending and need to be treated with caution. For some children these games can over-stimulate them and make them harder to manage. This sort of physical contact may seem to be the only thing that they enjoy and there may be a place for it but, as they get other attention, their need for this kind of contact generally reduces.

16. **Avoid activities that cannot be done by the child on their own.**

    Some activities are less well suited to attending. Do not let your child choose activities like board games or reading for this special time. Board games can present problems. Children need to learn how to deal with winning and losing but this is not the aim of attending. Helping children to read is also important but it can easily turn the parent into a teacher rather than a supporter. Colouring books, although developing co-ordination skills, are also not ideal as they do not encourage creativity and children can easily feel that they have made a mistake, e.g. by going over a line, which can result in parents pointing out how to do it better.

17. **During the attending session try to ignore the things that you do not like your child to do.**

    Even if you help your child to choose a creative activity like play dough he or she may still do some things that you do not like, for example, using the play materials in an aggressive way. This is best dealt with by ignoring (see Chapter 5 on Ignoring), pick up a paper or magazine for a moment or two until the play returns to something that you like.

18. **You are in charge of how long the session lasts.**

    You must decide how long you have. Don't get trapped into attending for longer than you want or it will put you off finding time to do it the next day. Sometimes children make a fuss when you want to end the session but think of this as a compliment since it means that they have really valued your positive attention. There are several things that you can do to help your child to accept the end of the session. First you must give them a warning that there is only so much time left before you have to do something else. You need to think of the best way to convey time to your child depending on their age. It can be hands on the clock, just adding three more pieces to the Lego tower or using a timer that the child can set. Next, it is important to praise the child and let them know that you have enjoyed watching their play. Then you can let the child know that you can do it again tomorrow. Finally, you can let them know what you now need to do and what they can do. Giving a choice is ideal, you could say: "I need to get the tea now so you can carry on playing or come and help me." If you do all of these things your child will accept the end of the session and will often choose to come and help you, valuing your attention at least as much as the play activity.

19. Let things go at your child's pace.

Children need to do things in their own time, try to give them time, do not try to hurry them on. The aim of attending is to strengthen your relationship, not to complete a set task. Children also learn from, and enjoy, repetition – putting the bricks in and out of a box or building the same tower of bricks every day, for example. Whilst it may seem boring to an adult, they are developing co-ordination skills and confidence in their abilities.

20. **Look for opportunities to attend during every-day activities.**

A few toys and an extra five minutes of play in the bath can provide a great opportunity for attending. There may be other times like preparation for bedtime that provide an opportunity. It is also good to read to children at bedtime but this tends to be parent led and does not count as attending, although it is a very important thing to do for children's school readiness and language development. It is not attending, which is about building children's self-confidence through their own activities.

Conclusion

The benefits of attending are enormous. Attending makes children feel that they are valued in their own right. The feelings that we have about ourselves are a reflection of what we have learned from other people about our worth. When parents attend, their children respond to this. The fear that some parents have that their child will become disruptive if allowed to have control of the play session is usually not well founded. Attending also helps children to develop language and communication skills and, by our example, we are teaching them how to show an interest in others.

Encouraging children to play helps to develop their creativity and their understanding of the world. Many children spend too much of their time in passive activities, such as watching TV, and do not learn to feel confident in their own skills or pride in their own achievements. Attending is not a waste of time. All the evidence says that building a relationship with children through attending is an essential step in teaching them to want to do what is asked of them. A lot of children's lives are spent doing things that are more important to adults, like cleaning their teeth, getting ready for bed, etc. They will respond much more positively to instructions if they feel valued.

Attending gives parents a chance to learn a lot about their children's interests and abilities. The mum of a pair of "identical" twins only learned through attending how they were different, with each having some different interests and abilities from the other.

Finally, many parents have not got much money and worry about not being able to give their children all of the "things" that other children seem to have. But children do not need expensive toys and, by practicing attending, many parents have found that their time is worth a million dollars to their children. The suggestions above have helped many parents to strengthen their relationships with their children and provided a foundation for children to develop self-confidence and social and communication skills. Remember, "We are models for our children's behaviour." One mother who used these ideas with her eight-year-old reported that, after four weeks, her son said: "You are a lovely mummy." It was the first time that her son had ever said anything like this and it certainly demonstrated to her the power of her attending.

3 Praising and rewarding children's positive behaviour

Many things that we do, particularly how we get on with other people, are learned. Praise and rewards play an important part in this learning. Everything we do is more likely to happen again if it is rewarded in some way and the most powerful reward, particularly for young children, is positive attention. Behaviour that is ignored, or not rewarded, is less likely to happen again. So, it is important to reward children when they behave in ways that we would like to see them repeat. In thinking about how to encourage behaviour we want more of, we first need to remember that our positive attention will only be effective if we have invested in our relationship with our children, through attending to them and the things that matter to them, as described in Chapter 2. Once we start doing this, our positive attention becomes a powerful tool for helping children learn to do the things that we want them to do.

Because attention is such a powerful reward for young children, the main focus of this chapter is on what we call social rewards, such as praise, attention, smiles and gentle touch. Other rewards (such as prizes or activities) can also be useful and some of the other ways of rewarding children through using small incentives are also described. These can be particularly helpful for difficult or stuck behaviours. However, social rewards are most important, in fact babies look for, and interpret, positive attention from the time they are born.

Although our focus is on children, social rewards are also important to adults too, for example, when a person returns your greeting it is a small but important reward to you for having said hello to them. It lets you know that the other person is pleased that you have shown interest in them. We can use what we know about rewarding to help children learn to do things we would like them to do. Rewarding children for behaving in ways that we approve of will encourage them to behave again in those ways in the future. This is important, no matter how small the behaviour that we want to encourage might seem.

Five-year-old Andy's mother, Kate, did not notice when he was being helpful by passing toys to his baby brother. She made no comment on his helpful behaviour but when Andy was rough with him she reacted by scolding him. When Kate made a special effort to notice the times when Andy was being helpful things changed. When Andy was chatting in a friendly way with his brother Kate rewarded him by smiling at him and saying: "I'm glad that you are being friendly with your brother." Andy looked pleased, and continued to chat nicely for a further five minutes. When Andy was not being friendly to his brother Kate made sure that it was the baby who got her attention, rather than Andy. This combination of praising Andy for friendly behaviour and giving attention to the baby when Andy was not behaving appropriately soon changed Andy's behaviour.

With some children, especially those who have behavioural or developmental challenges, it can be difficult to spot positive behaviour and parents find themselves forced into the role of fire officer, putting out the flames when problems arise. It can be hard to remember to keep a close eye on these children and "catch" them doing the things we like to see them doing. To begin with we might have to reward them for the smallest things that they already do, such as putting their coat on, or sitting quietly at the table for two minutes. This will soon pay dividends as children start to show more of the behaviours that have been rewarded. To begin with we should praise all of the desired behaviours in our children. However, after a week or so we will not have to "catch" them every time, only often enough that they realise that we are noticing their positive behaviours. In time, children will behave in a positive way without our rewards, as they will have taken our values on board and will have learned to feel good about themselves for behaving in certain ways. The praise that they have received will have built their self-confidence and self-esteem. Babies are not born with self-esteem, it is something that is gradually internalised over time as a result of the messages that the world gives to children as they grow. As an added bonus for positive attention, children with good relationships with the adults around them also look for other things that they can do that will please them. They will also have expectations of positive relationships with other people and will behave in ways that encourage others to respond positively to them.

In everyday language, a reward is often thought of as a prize given for some important action, such as passing an exam, but in the way that we are talking about here we are simply talking about the effect that our behaviour achieves. If it gets a positive response it increases the likelihood that it will happen again and if it gets no response or a negative response it is unlikely to happen again. Sometimes we inadvertently reward unwanted behaviours by paying attention to them. Of course we have to attend to some problem behaviours, particularly if they are aggressive or dangerous, but we need to give four times more attention to positive behaviour if we want to see a reduction in problem behaviour.

There are other rules that help to make rewarding effective. For small children, when learning new behaviour, they need to be rewarded *immediately* to learn, but as they grow older most children learn to work for longer to achieve rewards such as working for exam success or developing complex skills that need practice and take time to learn. But it was probably the small immediate rewards that got them started, such as being praised for doing homework. As adults we may be rewarded at work through promotion, status and wage increases, and by friends through pleasant social interactions and demonstrations of friendship, care and trust.

For children who have difficulties, the process of working for longer term rewards can be hard to learn, so parents may need to persist for longer with small immediate rewards. Think of cleaning your teeth; probably no-one rewards you for doing it as an adult but you have internalised it and it is also part of your routine. However, it was probably encouragement and praise in the first place that helped you learn to do it.

Social rewards are the most effective and important rewards we can give to children (and adults too in many cases). Not only do they make the behaviours which we want to see happen more often, they also give children high self-esteem and promote their social skills through modelling these friendly behaviours. Remember "we are models for our children's behaviour".

What follows are ten rules on how to praise your child effectively

1. When your child behaves in a way that you like, or has done something that you want them to do, give praise straight away. Do not wait until later to praise them. "You are a star, you listened to me and got ready for bed straight away." You can also add a tangible reward, for example: "Now we will have time for an extra story at bedtime."

2. Give praise for a "specific" thing that your child has done, or for a specific way your child has behaved. Tell them what it was. "I like the way that you came to the table when I asked you."

3. Give your child your undivided attention when you are praising them.

4. Move close to your child to praise them. It is important that they know that your attention is for them.

5. Use your child's name when you praise them. That way your child will know that you are talking to them. This will also help when we come to discussing effective ways of giving instructions.

6. Back up your praise in other ways. Smile at your child so that they know that you are pleased with

them. Body language is at least as important as our words in conveying our feelings. Give your child a hug or other gentle touch, a rub on the back, a kiss or cuddle or a high five. Children are programmed from birth to respond to gentle touch. It will make them feel good about themselves.

7. Praise your child in front of other adults. They will know that you are proud of them and it will encourage other adults to do the same. You can tell your child's teacher or phone a relative or friend to share the good news: "Michael I am going to tell Granny what a good job you did getting ready for bed so quickly." "You will never believe what Janet did

today, she cleaned her teeth after breakfast without me having to remind her."

8. Never praise and criticise a child at the same time. Praise should be nothing but good. Don't spoil it with a comment like: "Why can't you do that every time?"

9. Use words that label feelings and share your own positive feelings about your child and their behaviour. "I like it when you ..." (tidy up when I ask you to, eat tidily, etc.) "It makes me feel really proud of you when ..."

10. Encourage children to praise themselves, as this is what we want them to do in the long term. Say something like: "I am really proud of you for sharing your toys, I bet you are proud of yourself too." Or: "Tell yourself that you have done a good job and been very friendly." In time this self-praise

will be sufficient as children learn to internalise these messages and it becomes part of their self-esteem that they feel good about their behaviour. Remember the more praise you give children the less they will need.

Here is a list of things you can say to reward your child:

"Thank you for ..." (putting the toys away, playing quietly when I was talking, laying the table, etc.)

"You've done a good job of ..." (putting your socks on, building the bricks, etc.)

"Good boy for ..." (sitting down when I asked you to, fetching the baby wipes, etc.)

"Well done!"

"I'm very happy that you ..." (had fun doing that jig-saw, did as I asked you, etc.)

"Great! Wonderful! Brilliant! Perfect!" "Look how
well you …"

"I am really proud of you for …" "I'm really pleased
that you …" "I like playing with you."

"That was a very friendly thing to do."

"That was difficult and you were so patient."

Giving small rewards or incentives for positive behaviour

Many of the rules for giving rewards are similar to
those for giving effective praise, but there are two
ways to reward children; the first is to give
a spontaneous or unplanned reward: "You got ready
for bed so quickly that there is time for an extra
story". This is particularly suitable for younger children. For older children it can be helpful to use
planned rewards. These are things that your child
might like to have, such as stickers, toys or special
treats, being allowed to do something special at home
or choosing to do an activity outside your home.
Rewards should not be expensive and many can be
free, like going to the park to play, having some extra
special time together or having a friend to tea. Small
rewards can be useful to help a child to learn something that takes time, so, for an older child, you might
give a special reward after earning five stars. However,
it is important to always praise children when giving
a tangible reward, and to be sure to label what they
have done that pleases you.

Reward your child with the things that they like. It is a good idea to make a list of some of the things that your child likes, for example, activities and toys. You can then use the list to remind you of things you can use as rewards. These should be inexpensive. Sometimes you can turn things your child already has into rewards by giving extra time in a favourite activity. It is not the material value of the reward that is important, but rather it is its rewarding value. If you give small rewards from the start and make your child feel pleased about receiving them by praising them as well, they will not expect expensive rewards. We all like material possessions, and money can certainly make life easier, but praise is still the most effective way to encourage behaviour because of the relationship skills it develops. An added bonus is that since "we are models for our children's behaviour" it makes it more likely that our children will also praise others.

Examples of small rewards

- sticking a star on a star chart
- crayons, stickers, etc.
- small sums of money, for example twenty pence
- choosing a favourite cereal or biscuit when shopping or a pudding for dinner
- a special snack after school
- having a friend over to play or for a sleepover
- choosing what to have for tea
- going to the park/going on a picnic
- going swimming
- an extra bedtime story
- doing a jigsaw with you
- having an extra five minutes playtime

- helping a parent with a special task, cooking something together
- listening to a favourite tape or watching a DVD

Six rules for giving rewards

Many of these rules are similar to those for giving effective praise, but the following six rules mainly apply to planned rewards, so are for older children.

1. Make the target behaviour absolutely clear to both yourself and your child. Get the child to tell you what the plan is. "If you put the toys away when I ask, you will get a star and when you have five stars, you can have a friend to tea".

2. Make sure that the chosen behaviour is something that the child can do. A reward is only effective if the child gets it. If they do not get it because the target is too vague or too difficult for them to achieve, like being good all morning, this will be a negative experience for the child. Unfortunately, parents often say things like this without explaining what being good means and with a time scale that is unrealistic. Playing quietly with your sister for five minutes might be a lot more effective, because it is possible, than being good all morning.

3. Make sure that the reward is something that the child wants. If they do not want it they will not work for it. Some parents set up a menu with their children.

4. Remember to give the reward at the agreed time. Like praise it is important that rewards are as immediate as possible. When a child has earned a reward they must have it as soon as the required behaviour has been achieved. "You have done your homework so now you can play on your computer." Even if the reward is earned for behaviour over time you must monitor it and ensure that you give the reward once it has been earned. This is something that parents can forget after a while when the desired behaviour is becoming established. You will not have to reward it for life but it is good to be clear about the end of the reward system. "You are so good at cleaning your teeth now that I think we could change things so that you earn your extra computer time for putting your dirty washing in the laundry basket."

5. Always give praise with the reward, it makes your praise more effective by association with the reward. "You did a great job putting the toys away. I am really proud of you." And of course all the earlier rules about praise apply too, specific, immediate, enthusiastic, etc..

6. Target one behaviour at a time and ideally do not choose the most difficult behaviour first. You want the child to experience the benefits of working for a reward before tackling more "stuck" behaviours and, even when you do, you need to make sure the goal is achievable, such as "sitting at the table for five minutes".

Other things to think about with praise and rewards

Some parents feel embarrassed about praising and rewarding children. We may have few experiences of praise or positive attention ourselves, so lack positive role models. Praising, however, becomes easier each time that we do it and it is also rewarded by the response that it gets for us from our children. Once parents get used to rewarding they find that it becomes an easy and natural way of letting their children know that their behaviour is approved of and it becomes a very effective way of increasing that behaviour.

Rewarding a child for appropriate behaviour is showing that you approve of that behaviour. Even though we are not always aware of it, it is something that has influenced all of us. By planning and using rewarding systematically we are consciously using a natural response to encourage appropriate behaviour. We are in control of the learning situation in a way that is helpful to both parents and children.

Rewarding makes children more independent

Some parents feel that children should be motivated to do things without being rewarded and that they might become dependent on rewards, and not behave in the way we want them to unless given a reward. In fact, the opposite is true. Children who are rewarded for their behaviour become less dependent on their parents' praise and rewards as they grow older and become more independent and self-motivated. They take on board the positive views of themselves and behave in positive ways because it becomes how they see themselves.

Rewards must come after the behaviour we want

There is a difference between bribing and rewarding. In our society we think of bribes as things that are given or offered when one person is trying to make another person behave in an illegal or unethical way. Furthermore, they are often given before the required behaviour. It is important to remember that you must always reward after the behaviour you want has occurred. Do not reward your child before they have behaved in a way that you want, even if you think that there is a very good chance that your child is going to do it. If you have asked your child to put the toys away and said that they will have a biscuit when the job is done, you must give your child the biscuit only when all of the toys have been put away and not before (remembering to give praise as well, of course!). If your child says: "If you let me watch this programme now I will do my homework afterwards," you may have trouble getting them to do it. It is more effective to record the programme for them to watch later when the home-work is done and you will not have to nag them later to do it. Nagging is the opposite of rewarding since children only do what we ask to stop the nagging and we may find that we have to nag more and more as time goes by to get the desired behaviour. This carries the other risk of having a negative effect on our relationship with our children, because when we have to repeat what we want children to do we tend not to do it in the most positive way: "How many times must I tell you …" Remember, "we are models for our children's behaviour".

Other benefits of using praise and rewards

When parents reward children for good behaviour, they will also be rewarded by their children. If children are behaving in the way that we want, we are much more relaxed, friendly and calm. It can be embarrassing when a child is behaving inappropriately in front of friends or

family, so by using a strategy to encourage good behaviour, visiting friends can be a more pleasant experience. Many parents have reported that their homes have become happier and calmer places and that they feel less stressed when they pay more attention to their children's good behaviour.

Children imitate the behaviour around them, whether they are aware of it or not. We encourage this from the time children are born. When we praise children the chances are that they will also start praising their friends and brothers and sisters. Giving positive attention to their peers will make our children fun to be with, and popular. When parents get good at giving praise they sometimes find that their partner, family and friends, start to give praise and positive attention for behaviour that might have gone unnoticed in the past. So we can find that "we are models for other people" as well as for our children.

In order to help learning, consequences need, at first, to be immediate and frequent but gradually we learn to do things for longer-term goals. However, when we learn to do things for more distant goals, this is usually because there were immediate consequences helping us to learn. We were praised for doing home-work etc.

A parent who is teaching a child to save some of his sweets for later in the day praises him for doing it, or a parent who is teaching a child to save her pocket money praises her and talks to her about the benefits of saving. The parent is therefore giving immediate attention to the child for learning to wait for other rewards. Many consequences that influence our lives as adults are longer term, things like pay, studying for exams, child rearing or taking on mortgages. The behaviours that are required in order to achieve each of these goals are usually far more likely to occur when the person is being helped to plan for such goals. Even in adult life, many of the consequences that influence our behaviour are immediate or short-term ones. For example, an adult who gives in to a child's tantrums because the tantrum stops may recognise that they are failing to help the child to learn self-control. However, they may find it difficult to do otherwise because the immediate consequence of the cessation of the tantrum rewards the parent.

Conclusion

By getting praise and other positive attention regularly, children's self-esteem increases. Children who have high self-esteem will be less dependent on their parents, grow up with feelings of satisfaction and confidence and develop positive relationships with others around them. This is what all parents want for their children but it only happens with planning and practice by parents.

4 How to get better at giving instructions

It is very important to help children to learn to follow instructions because this is something that will help them to cope well in many other situations, particularly in school. Many parents have problems getting children to follow instructions. In fact most children only follow about 75% of the instructions that they are given by their parents and most of us accept that as being good enough. Children who have difficulty in following instructions generally follow more instructions than we realise, although this is often less than half of the instructions that they receive. We also know

that children who have difficulty in following instructions tend to receive more instructions than well-behaved children. Unfortunately, when a child has difficulty in following instructions we tend to look for, and notice, when they fail to follow them and it can be easy to miss the times when they do as they are told. There are a number of common mistakes made by parents when giving instructions but careful attention to how we give instructions can make it more likely that children will follow them. This chapter describes common problems and difficulties and gives a set of rules about how to improve the way that we give instructions.

Typical problems

1 **Giving too many instructions**

Parents of children who find it hard to follow instructions usually give large numbers of instructions. This can be many hundreds of instructions in an hour. However, the number of instructions that are actually followed by the child can be very few indeed. One mother of a hyperactive three-year-old gave 67 instructions in a short space of time, none of which were followed by the child. In fact some of her instructions caused problems to occur. When he was near the TV his mum said: "Don't touch the TV," and he immediately touched it.

2 **Instructions are too general**

Instructions are often much too general such as:

"Be good", "Tidy your room" or "Use your manners". For an obedient or compliant child these may be quite acceptable instructions because they have learned what we mean by these things, but for a child who has difficulty following instructions they are too vague. Being good might mean playing in a friendly way with your sister instead of grabbing her toys, keeping your hands to yourself instead of hitting someone, playing quietly with the bricks rather than throwing them around the room, talking in a quiet voice rather than shouting. So, to help some children to learn to follow instructions we have to be much more specific and tell them exactly what we want them to do.

3 **Negative instructions**

Another problem is that instructions are often phrased negatively. The parent says: "Stop doing that" or "Don't do that", rather than directing their child to do something else. It is better to give a specific instruction that will interfere with what a child is doing. So, instead of saying: "Stop climbing on the settee" you could say "Please come over here".

4 **Repeated instructions**

Parents of children who find instruction following difficult can find themselves repeating instructions because they think the child did not hear them the first time. However, giving the child time to process an instruction can be more effective. Some children take time to respond and repeated instructions can add to the problem because the child learns that the parent will say it again. This teaches

the child that they do not have to do it the first time that they hear the instruction. An unfortunate consequence of repeating instructions is that parents tend to repeat them in an ever more negative way out of frustration: "Why can't you do it the first time I ask you ..." This results in an unpleasant atmosphere for the parent and the child.

5   **Giving too many instructions at once**
Parents can give a string of instructions. For example, "Get yourself up, washed and dressed. Put a clean vest on and don't forget to clean your teeth." Whilst we do want children to learn to follow this string of actions that comprise their morning routine, this is not a very effective way of teaching this routine. It is far more successful, in

the early stages, to give one instruction at a time followed by praise.

6 **Failure to follow through with instructions by parents**

Parents can give an instruction but then become distracted from following it through. This can be for several reasons. The simplest reason may be that the phone rings, the baby cries and the instruction is forgotten. Children can frequently distract their parents by challenging the instruction and setting up a debate: "Why should I?", "You didn't make my brother do that", "My friend doesn't have to go to bed at 8 o'clock" etc. Some parents have learned to expect such challenges and then start to justify why the instruction should be followed. This can lead to long discussions and negotiations, which can be unhelpful and unnecessary. Children do need explanations and a chance to discuss things, but there is a time and place for this and it is not when giving a specific instruction and definitely not every time the same instruction is given.

7 **Parental body language and non-verbal messages say: "I do not think that you will do this"**

Probably as a result of difficulties in the past in getting their child to follow instructions, sometimes a parent's tone of voice and body language when giving instructions tells the child that the parent does not expect them to comply. It is not uncommon for parents initially to give an instruction in a half-hearted way, hardly expecting the child to do as they are told. When, as expected, the child does not obey the parent can become angry with the child in an attempt to get them to follow the instruction or simply give up.

8   **Failure to get the child's attention**

Some parents give instructions without first getting the child's attention. The child may be busy doing something, such as watching television, and the parent may fail to get the child to acknowledge, by looking or answering, that they are listening to the instruction. You might need to turn the TV off.

9   **Instructions may sound like a choice**

Sometimes we fail to recognise that there are two options, either we tell a child to do something or we give them a choice. It can be very confusing to a child when instructions are given in a way that suggests that there is a choice when this is not intended. For example, if the toys must be put away it is not helpful to say: "Are you going to put your toys away?" "Would you like to put your toys away?" or "Shall we put the toys away?" The child can answer "No", to all of these questions and that then makes it hard for you to insist on the job being done. For children who have learned to follow instructions these rather vague choice instructions can be successful. "It is almost bedtime so would you like to put your toys away now and get ready for your bath?" will work for some children but it is not helpful for a child who is still learning to follow instructions.

10 **Rules are applied inconsistently**

In relation to family or household rules, it is important to be consistent. It is not helpful to allow children to climb on the settee sometimes, then decide at a different time that this is not acceptable and shout at the child, saying for example, "How many times have I told you not to climb on the settee?" It is important for the child to know what the household rules are and that they apply all of the time and parents must notice immediately when the child needs reminding.

11 Threats are made but not carried out

Another problem is the use of threats which parents make in an attempt to get children to follow instructions that they either cannot, or do not, carry out. From November onwards many children hear: "If you don't do as you are told then Father Christmas won't come." Children rapidly learn that such threats are meaningless and, in any case, if consequences are needed (something that is discussed in Chapter 6), the same rule applies as for positive attention. That is, immediate consequences are much more likely to be successful.

12 Failure to give the child preparation time before the instruction

This is a common problem where the child is engaged in an activity and the instruction seems to come from nowhere. Children need time to process an instruction and finish what they are doing, especially those who have challenging behaviours. We have already discussed this idea in Chapter 2, in talking about warning children about when special time will end. Children need to have a warning that the instruction will follow shortly.

Twenty rules to increase children's willingness to follow instructions

The following rules help avoid some of the common pitfalls described above and increase children's willingness to follow instructions.

1. Give one instruction at a time and then praise the child with a specific, labelled praise when they complete it.

2. Remember to make the instruction positive and specific. Instructions should be given to do something rather than to stop doing something, to use quiet walking feet indoors; speak with a quiet indoor voice. These instructions give messages that

running and shouting are not wrong but do not happen in certain places.

3. Acknowledge the difficulty: "I know that you are enjoying playing with the blocks but it will soon be time to get ready for bed so please put the toys away now. You can play with them again tomorrow." "Thank you for …"

4. Share your own positive feelings with your child when they follow instructions. "I am proud of you …"

5. Reduce the number of instructions that you give overall. Decide first: "Do I have to give this instruction?" If it does not really matter do not give it.

6. Give the child time to prepare for the instruction. We call this a "transition warning". Tell the child how long they have left to play and then follow

through with the instruction. If your child is playing or watching TV give a five minute warning. "In five minutes time it will be time to pack up the toys and get ready for bed," and then after five minutes give the instruction and stay with it until the child complies.

7. Once you give the instruction you must follow it through, do not give up or be distracted and do not debate the rule. Give the child time to comply before repeating the request. An instruction should generally be given only twice before you follow through with a gesture or a gentle physical prompt, such as gently taking the child's hand that says that you mean it. We describe how to deal with "stuck" problems with instruction following in Chapter 6.

8. Make sure that you give the instruction in a way that sounds as if you expect the child to do it. This is about the tone of voice and body language. Give the instruction in a pleasant but assertive way and stay calm so that the child knows that you expect them to do it. Do not raise your voice. When you know that you are going to follow it through, you know that you are in control and can remain calm when giving an instruction. Behave all the time as if you expect the child to do what you ask. The instruction should be given in a firm voice that suggests to the child that you expect them to comply.

9. Once the child has done what you ask, praise them, even if they have done it reluctantly, perhaps swearing or shouting, for example, or throwing the toys into the box. Do not mention the problem behaviour, only the fact that the child did what they were told. "Thank you for putting the toys in the box."

10. Have action replays for good behaviour – remind the child of good things that they have done and tell other people when the child is there. Never remind the child of problem behaviour. If you have to deal with problem behaviour, which we deal with in Chapter 6, the rule is to deal with it but not to revisit it.

11. Give lots of instructions that you know the child will want to follow. For example, "Come here and get this ice-cream" or "Put your coat on to go to the park" or "Put your toys away so that we can go for a pizza". Remember to praise the child for

following the instructions, in addition to the specific praise you can say: "You are so good at doing what I ask".

12. Give the child instructions to do things that they are just about to do so that they are following instructions without realising it. For example, "That's right put the bubble bath into the water" or "Yes open the gate for Granny to come in".

13. If a child is unlikely to follow an instruction, e.g. to stop running away, it is better not to give the instruction. Go to the child and physically make sure, if at all possible, that they do what you want and are safe. Do not give an instruction that you know that a child will disobey. There is no point in giving them practice in refusing to follow instructions.

14. Whilst you are helping your child to learn to follow instructions avoid situations that are difficult to control, like supermarket shopping trips. Help them to learn to follow instructions at home first. You can play a make-believe shopping trip to practice how you want them to behave in the supermarket, holding on to the trolley, helping you to find things, choosing a cereal etc.

15. Get the child's attention before giving an instruction. This often involves moving close to them, saying their name and getting them to look at you before giving the instruction. "Peter I need you to look at me please so that I can tell you what we are doing this morning."

16. If an explanation is necessary give it before the instruction so that the instruction is the last thing that the child hears. For example, "We are going to visit Granny shortly so I would now like you to put away the Lego please".

17. Decide on the house rules and agree them with your partner or other household members, then stick to them. If the rule is, "Drinks only at the table", this must always be the rule for all of the family, or not at all. Have few but clear household rules that apply to everyone. State the rules positively, such as using friendly language, eating meals at the table or using gentle hands.

18. In some situations we can give a child a choice, "When you have done your homework then you can watch TV." But if they choose not to do the

homework you have to follow through and ensure no TV. Children rapidly learn that we mean what we say but remember to stay calm when you give the choice and if you have to, remind the child why they cannot watch TV. You can also say that they will be able to watch TV tomorrow when they have done their homework

19. If you are giving an instruction to more than one child, remember to praise the child that complies rather than giving your attention to the one that has not yet followed the instruction. We call this "proximal praise", ensuring that praise for behaviour we want gets more attention than the behaviour that we do not want. This can be remarkably effective, especially if you have been attending and building your relationship with your children because the other child will also want to be in the sunshine of your positive attention.

20. Remember children will want to follow our instructions if we have a good relationship with

them at other times, remember the importance of play and relationship building at other times when you are not giving instructions.

Conclusion

Everything takes time and patience, but parents who take time to play with their children and follow these rules about how to get better at giving instructions report great success in helping their children learn an important social skill which will help them in many situations.

5 Ignoring problem behaviour

Children's need for attention is established very early in their life. If it is not given freely they work hard to get it. This is true for all of us but attention is a particularly powerful reward when children are young because they are programmed to seek it. So focusing too much attention on problem behaviour can accidentally teach children to do more and more of the very things we do not want them to do.

If children get plenty of attention for just being themselves, as well as for the "good" things they do, it helps them to feel good about themselves and

generally they also want to please adults and do what they are asked. If children do not get enough attention for positive behaviour, from the people who matter to them, they soon discover other ways to get the attention that they need. Problem behaviours can include whining, demanding, swearing, tantrumming, showing off and lots of other undesirable behaviours.

Ian was a disobedient and disruptive child, whose mother came for help in managing his many problem behaviours. He also had a habit of sniffing, and this irritated his mother. Every few minutes, sometimes several times in one minute, Ian's mother interrupted her conversation to say: "Stop sniffing, Ian!" or "Don't sniff!" Ian did not have a cold, and it was possible that he had learned to sniff because it had got his mother's attention at a time when he did have a cold. Because his behaviour was challenging for much of the time, his mother did not find him much fun to be with and gave him little positive attention for just being himself. She started by learning to give positive attention to Ian and to praise and reward him but, at the same time, she started ignoring Ian's sniffing.

What do we mean by ignore? We mean not speaking about the behaviour, not appearing to hear or see it, acting as if it hasn't happened. Sometimes it means walking out of the room or reminding ourselves that this is what children do for attention. This is very difficult to do, we seem to be "programmed" to notice and intervene when problems occur. We do this to try to

help children to learn but sometimes children learn the wrong lesson from our attention.

When his mother started to ignore Ian's sniffing it seemed to get worse for the first few hours but, within a week, it had become so rare that she heard it only a couple of times in a whole day. Ian's mother had found it very difficult to ignore. She found herself tensing up, and being tempted to shout about it but she persevered and was delighted that it was working. This confirmed the idea that Ian's sniffing was probably occurring because of his mother's attention. However, because she was now noticing and rewarding his good behaviour as well as ignoring the sniffing, her strategy paid off.

Ignoring only works if the child is provided with more acceptable ways to gain attention, otherwise ignoring

a problem can result in an even more troublesome behaviour that we cannot ignore. So, used together with praise and rewards, ignoring can be a powerful tool which parents can use to reduce some of their children's unwanted behaviour.

When a new baby arrives, an older child may resent the fact that he or she doesn't get as much attention as they were used to. This happened to Matthew – he was jealous. Like many jealous children, he discovered that he could get his mother's attention all to himself again, and away from his brother, by pinching the baby. His mother reacted by scolding him, but, by doing that, she was giving him attention. It may seem hard to understand, but attention is so important to children that, in a situation like this, they can prefer to have unpleasant attention, such as scolding, than no attention at all.

Matthew's mother was surprised when told to ignore Matthew when he pinched the baby, but, instead, to give lots of attention to the baby. She was told to pick up the baby and walk out of the room with him. This was the opposite of what Matthew was expecting! In addition, his mother was told to give Matthew extra attention when he was playing nicely near the baby and to talk to him and involve him when she was changing or feeding the baby. It was also important that she gave Matthew some special time on his own when the baby was sleeping. Within two weeks there was no longer a problem and Matthew was behaving caringly towards his younger brother. This would not be the right approach for a child who hurt the baby when the parents were out of sight. Ignoring means removing attention, so it only works when the reward is immediate parental attention. A child that hurts another child when no-one else is present is also indicating that they have some unmet needs, but these would need to be dealt with in another way. In that situation the first concern would be to remove the opportunity and ensure that the child is not left alone with the other child until the problem can be understood and dealt with.

When a parent uses ignoring to reduce a particular behaviour it can get worse for a while. It is as if the child can't believe what is happening so they try harder with the behaviour that has been rewarded in the past. It is a bit like a fruit machine where, if you do not win, you put more money in because you are never quite sure when it will pay off. However, as long as the parent is consistent, usually after quite a short while the behaviour starts to decrease. It generally reduces very quickly, especially if parents are giving the child other ways of getting attention. Behaviour that has had a pay-off every time is generally easier to get rid of than behaviour that is only rewarded occasionally. When the reward stops it disappears very quickly.

Unfortunately, many problem behaviours are not rewarded every time. It is a bit like buying a lottery ticket; the lottery will pay out to somebody and we may be one of the lucky ones this week. In the same way much of our behaviour occurs not because it gets the expected reward every time but because it gets a pay-off from time to time. Behaviour that has only been rewarded occasionally can be more difficult to deal with than behaviour that is rewarded every time, precisely because it was not rewarded every time and what had been learned was that it might be next time. So, it takes persistence and ignoring has to be even more consistent to deal with a problem like that.

If possible, everybody in the family should agree to ignore a particular behaviour and carry it out. If there are other children around they can be taught to ignore and praised for helping their brother or sister by ignoring the problem behaviour. Sometimes, when parents are ignoring one child another child will say, "Mum he is doing it again," but if a parent replies by saying, "I am glad that you are playing carefully with the toys, you are

I am glad that you are playing nicely with your brother.

a good example to your brother," it can help the other child learn not to give attention to the problem. This can also help the child whose behaviour is being ignored by reminding them indirectly what behaviour gets attention.

Once a decision has been made to ignore a particular behaviour it is important to be consistent and make sure the reward does not happen. Sometimes people decide to ignore difficult behaviour and manage on a few occasions, but are then unable to keep this up. Maybe they are embarrassed because they have a visitor so they tell the child off or maybe give the attention that the child is asking for to keep them quiet. So, the child learns that sometimes their behaviour produces attention and they may repeat the behaviour again many times until it is rewarded again. It takes a lot more for the child to learn that this behaviour is never going to be rewarded than if the behaviour has been rewarded every time. If parents decide to ignore a particular behaviour they have to be sure that they can carry it through. This may mean explaining to visitors what they are doing and why, or even stopping having visitors for a while. Some parents have trouble getting others to ignore a particular behaviour. Ideally everyone should ignore. However, if one person is consistent in themselves, even if others are not, children learn how to respond to that person and if that person is a key person in the child's life it will still be effective and also provide a great example to other people because "we are models to other people around us".

Successful ignoring works when attention is the reward for the behaviour. Behaviours like arguing, sulking, screaming, interrupting, swearing and spitting, can be unhelpful ways of trying to get attention and may respond to ignoring. You cannot ignore behaviours that achieve other rewards. Refusal to obey instructions, for example, is generally not done for attention so will not respond to ignoring. Raiding the cupboard for biscuits, stealing money from Mum's handbag or coming home late will require other strategies and these are discussed in Chapter 6.

The other key point to remember when deciding to ignore a particular behaviour is whether the child has the skills to get the attention in a better way and whether the parents remember to reward positive behaviour four times more often than ignoring the problem behaviour. Maybe the problem behaviour is happening because getting attention in a different way is too difficult for the child.

Here are ten rules that will help to make ignoring successful:

1. Give no attention, either verbal or non-verbal. Do not speak or give eye contact. Ignoring is easier if we have decided what we are going to do whilst ignoring. It is important to have self-talk that reminds us why we are doing it. "If I keep ignoring this behaviour it will help my child to learn." It may help to walk to another room or keep moving if the child follows. Start to prepare a meal or sing a song.

2. As soon as the child's behaviour changes remember to return your attention to the child. You must ignore the behaviour not the child.

3. Decide if it is safe to ignore. You must also always respond to dangerous or destructive behaviours. Even though attention might be part of the pay-off for these behaviours you need another approach, see Chapter 6 on managing difficult behaviour.

4. Expect the problem to get worse at first when you ignore. This applies to any behaviour but particularly to behaviours that were only rewarded occasionally.

5. Ignoring must be done consistently or you can make the problem worse. It involves not allowing the child to get any direct response. You must not

reply to anything that is said and must try to give no eye contact.

6. Ignoring problem behaviours should ideally be done by everyone. Sometimes other people can respond when you are ignoring, so try to make sure that no-one gives attention to a behaviour that you are trying to stop. This means making a plan and talking with others about it. However, if you are the key person in the child's life, ignoring will work for you if you are consistent, even if other people do not do the same, and will make you a great model.

7. Be sure to reward other behaviours instead, at other times of the day, otherwise the child is likely to escalate their behaviour to force parents to respond. It is particularly helpful if you can reward a behaviour that is in contrast to the problem behaviour, like rewarding talking with a quiet voice

whilst ignoring shouting, being gentle or careful with toys or being friendly to a brother or sister.

8. Keeping a record of what is happening can be a useful strategy as it shows whether the problem is changing. If it gets worse then the child is telling you that it is your attention that is influencing the behaviour. Remember to tell yourself: "It is getting worse so my attention must be the reward. I need to help my child to learn a better way to get my attention."

9. Remember to praise other children who are behaving well when one child is misbehaving. Children quickly learn what gets our attention.

10. Start with only one behaviour as you must ignore the behaviour not the child. If you ignore too many different behaviours at once the child will not get enough positive attention and ignoring will not be effective.

Conclusion

Ignoring is difficult to do consistently but it is a powerful tool. Plan carefully before you begin. If you know you will give in after a while, do not use ignoring. If you do decide to ignore a behaviour make sure that the child has lots of positive ways to get attention and that some of the attention is for the opposite behaviour to that which is being ignored. Also remember the key rule is that the child must get four times as much attention for positive behaviour as they get for problem behaviour and that you must return your attention as soon as the problem behaviour stops. "Ignore a behaviour, not a child."

6 Managing difficult behaviours

For young, pre-school children you will not need to use the strategies described in this chapter because a combination of the strategies in the previous four chapters will be effective. The most important thing to remember in managing children's difficult behaviour is to make sure that they get at least four times more attention for positive behaviour than they do for problem behaviour. The second important thing to remember is to be consistent in managing both positive and problem behaviour. In terms of managing problem behaviour this means when a child does not do what we ask we must respond in the same way each time. This is the best and quickest way to help children learn. This also applies to positive attention, praise and ignoring.

This chapter is about how to deal with "stuck" behaviours or problems that have persisted for some time or behaviours that are dangerous for the child or for others. Even hitting is not dangerous if we are talking about a frustrated toddler who is hitting your legs because he cannot have a biscuit. Walking away and ignoring will work, but for older children the following strategies can be helpful.

Time to think

One way to deal with stuck problems is using a method known as time-out or quiet chair time, the other is to provide a consequence. Both are described in this chapter. Time-out has a bad reputation and many people have tried it unsuccessfully, so it is important to follow the quiet chair steps described in this chapter as they have been proved to be effective. The name quiet chair or thinking chair also helps the child to understand its purpose.

Quiet chair

It is important to think of time on the quiet chair as a structured ignore. It is a brief time away from the enjoyable things in life and involves removing the child from the situation for a short time, not more than five minutes, and then the child can return. Many parents who have tried using time-out found that it did not work and that problems persisted. This is because they were generally failing to follow one or two of the essential quiet chair rules. There are a number of things that have been shown to make quiet chair time work effectively. If you follow the instructions exactly and consistently, and if you give high rates of praise for positive behaviour, it will be effective in managing your child's problem behaviour even if you have previously used time out unsuccessfully.

When you start using quiet chair time, you will generally be doing something about your child's refusal to follow instructions or aggressive behaviour much sooner than you previously did. Even though the rule is to only target one problem at a time, you may have to use it quite frequently. If you use quiet chair time properly and consistently, it is unusual for high levels of use to continue for as long as a week.

By following the steps described here many parents have seen a very positive improvement within one week following setting up a quiet chair routine and also rewarding the alternative desired behaviours with at least four times as much "time in the sunshine of positive attention".

There are two situations where quiet chair time is useful:

i) Breaking a household rule. Quiet chair time can be used in situations where children disobey a rule that has previously been explained to them. For example, if there is a family rule of no hitting and

Thinking Chair

the child hits a sibling, parent or another person. In this case at the end of the quiet chair time the problem is not referred to but the child is simply invited back and praised for their first positive behaviour.

ii) Refusing to follow instructions. If the child is sent to the quiet chair for refusing to follow any instructions at the end of their time on the chair they must be asked again to carry out the instruction that had previously been given. This is important as children must not be able to use the quiet chair to avoid doing things that they would rather not do.

First, some general rules for quiet chair time are described and then suggestions as to how to deal with the two different types of problems.

General rules for quiet chair time:

1. You should only introduce quiet chair time for one problem at a time. Once that is solved, generally fairly quickly, you can use it for a different problem.
2. Quiet chair time must always be in contrast to the positive situation of "Time in the sunshine of positive attention", which is where the child needs to be for most of the time.
3. The child must be told, in advance, at a calm time about the quiet chair plan and it must be introduced as a helpful idea to solve one problem.
4. Make sure that you are teaching your child the behaviours needed to avoid using the quiet chair, for example, praising the child when they follow instructions, for using gentle hands or being friendly to their brother.
5. The quiet chair time must happen every time the child refuses to follow the instruction or breaks the known family rule, such as for an aggressive act.
6. Do not argue or reason with the child about why this happens. Many children are experts at engaging in debate about whether or not to do something. They generally find that discussion or argument is a very effective way of avoiding following instructions and getting their own way.
7. When the child needs to go to the quiet chair your manner should be entirely matter of fact. You know

what you are going to do and therefore you are in control of the situation. This will enable you to deal with it without becoming cross. You must state the reason briefly and then say, "You forgot the rule of gentle hands you must go to the quiet chair".

8. Do not threaten your child with the quiet chair. Once you have said "go to the quiet chair", you need to stick to it. Once you have started to carry out the quiet chair procedure do not backtrack because your child starts following instructions after the deadline or apologises for hitting, it is too late, they must go to the quiet chair.

9. Ideally, the quiet chair at first needs to be quite specific, a definite chair, cushion or mat. Many parents have found the bottom step of the stairs to be an ideal place, near to the parent but far enough away to be ignored and, most importantly, generally not very interesting for the child. The child's bedroom is not a good place since it is usually full of interesting things for the child to do, quiet chair time is "time away from rewarding activities". A good strategy is to have a chair or mat that you can move about so that you can put it in the corner of the kitchen if you are working there or because you cannot leave the child in the living room because someone else is watching TV.

10. Whilst the child is on the quiet chair they should have no verbal or physical contact with anybody. This means that whatever the child is doing you should not speak to him or her. You should ignore

threats or promises of "I will do as I am told", until the specified period has ended. Do not reply to anything that is said by the child, some of which may be aimed to hurt you.

11. When you first use the quiet chair routine, especially if your child makes a fuss or gets off the chair, you can say once, "Remember the time only starts when you are sitting quietly on the chair." If the child finds it difficult to calm down remind them once that the time will not finish until they are quiet.

12. The parent decides when it is over and not the child. Generally three minutes is sufficient for younger children, say three and four-year-olds, and five minutes for children over the age of five. Some people find it useful to have a kitchen timer that the child can observe, but not reach, which rings at the end of the quiet chair period. Not touching the clock can be made a rule.

13. A child must not leave the quiet chair if they are making a fuss or misbehaving when the time period finishes. The child must have been quiet for at least 30 seconds, and ideally two minutes, leading up to the end of the quiet chair period.

14. When the time on the chair is finished do not start a discussion with the child about why the child was sent there. This can make it less effective and we want the child to learn as quickly as possible. We know that the approach is working when you find that you are not needing to use it so much and then, finally, not at all.

15. If you are still using the quiet chair regularly for the same problem after a few weeks revisit the

Thinking Chair

steps, because that means that it is not working. Either the child is not getting enough "time in the sunshine of positive attention", or they do not have the skills to avoid the problem. So, you need to rethink and decide how to help your child to avoid the quiet chair by revisiting the earlier chapters.

Using the quiet chair for forgetting a rule

It is important that this is only used for problems that are dangerous for the child or others or are destructive. Other problems, such as swearing, can often be dealt with by ignoring or by a gentle reminder; "remember to use friendly words", which of course must then be praised.

1. Introduce the plan to the child as a way of helping the child to remember the rule.
2. If a child hits they must be told immediately, "You forgot the rule, you need to go to the quiet chair". They do not get a warning.
3. Once on the chair all of the other rules about it are the same as those for ignoring.

4. When the time is over say, "Your time on the chair is over now," and re-engage the child in a positive activity. Praise their first positive behaviour. Do not remind them of why they went to the chair because quiet chair time is a structured "ignore", and so it is important not to revisit the problem.

Rules for using the quiet chair to teach a child to follow instructions

1. Give the instruction, remember to follow all the rules in Chapter 4 on "How to get better at giving instructions".
2. If the instruction is not followed within five seconds it should be repeated with the addition of, "If you do not do what I asked now you will have to go to the quiet chair". Remember to use the same words and speak slowly, clearly and firmly in case your child was not paying attention to you the first time. If the child complies, praise them.
3. If your child does not comply, wait a further five seconds which you should count in your head. If the child has not followed your instruction in this time period say: "Go to the quiet chair". You must only say this once in a firm, but not cross, voice. Your manner should be entirely matter of fact. You know what you are going to do and therefore you are in control of the situation. This will enable you to deal with it without becoming cross.
4. If your child goes to the chair ignore them until the time is over and then say, "Your time on the

chair is over, please put the toys away now". It is important that they cannot use the quiet chair to avoid the instruction.

5. Remember to praise your child for following the instruction even if it is done with bad grace.

6. Remember that quiet chair time is only for refusing to follow an instruction or for doing something that the child knows that he or she is not allowed to do. You should have a list of house rules that lead to immediate time on the quiet chair for the child and explain them to your child at a quiet time. This list can be put up on a door or wall as a reminder to both of you.

Refusal to go to the quiet chair

If your child refuses to go or stay on the chair or mat there are several different ways of dealing with this, but again consistency of approach is needed. The way of dealing with younger children, is to return them to the chair each time they come off. You should do this without speaking and, as far as possible, without any further eye contact. You may have to repeat this a lot of times initially but if you do it without comment your child will learn to stay there until told to come from the chair.

If you cannot physically put your child on the chair because they are too big or too aggressive, you must use another approach – do not fight with your child to get them onto the chair because one of you might get hurt and also this is bad modelling, suggesting that "might is right".

One strategy is to repeat that the quiet chair time will not start until the child goes to the chair and then ignore them until they do go. Do not get drawn into any other conversation with the child and, at this point, all the rules of ignoring apply. Remember how powerful ignoring can be. Nothing else must happen for the child, no mealtimes or any other attention until the quiet chair time has taken place.

If you cannot ignore your child until they go to the chair, or if the child starts doing something dangerous that you cannot ignore, you must change strategy and give the child a choice. You must say, "You must go to the quiet chair or you will not be able to watch your TV programme this evening". You must plan a consequence in advance, preferably one that occurs quite soon, like losing half an hour of computer time the same evening. If the child does not go to the chair in five seconds you need to calmly say, "You have lost half an hour of your computer time this evening". Once a child has lost an important reward on one occasion they usually go to the chair the next time they are asked. So, following refusal, quiet chair time is given as a choice to do it or to take the consequence and the child will quickly learn to make the easiest and most sensible decision and go to the chair.

When to use consequences instead of quiet chair time

In some situations a brief time on the chair will not be effective, such as coming in later than agreed, taking food from the fridge, money from a purse or breaking something. These problems tend to occur with older children and young adolescents. In these cases a consequence must occur as soon as possible after the event by removing an opportunity to go out the next night, losing TV or computer time or losing a specific amount of pocket money to replace stolen money or to repair something.

Sometimes it is possible to teach children to put right the effects of what they have done wrong and to be responsible for their own behaviour. The parents of a child who had been knocking at people's doors and running away had received complaints from the neighbours. Instead of punishing the child for doing this they sat down and talked about the problem with the child. They agreed between them that the child should go back and apologise to the people who had been inconvenienced. The parents suggested that the child might say, "I hope that I didn't inconvenience you". The child responded that he obviously had inconvenienced the people and that it would be more appropriate to say, "I'm sorry I inconvenienced you". That child had learned a more valuable lesson than he might have done by simply being kept in, in order to avoid the problem occurring again. It had the added benefit that the people who received the apology probably ended up with better feelings towards the child than they would have done had he merely been punished by his parents.

A foster child argued with other children about what programme to watch on television. Initially, the parents adopted a strategy that involved switching off the television when the children were arguing, but they did not plan what they wanted instead. Their strategy led to their children not speaking to the foster child or saying things like, "I don't like you because you get me into trouble"; but this did not resolve the issue of how to agree which channel to watch. What worked was a strategy for teaching the children other ways of interacting. Once they did this, by sitting the children down together, defining the problem and looking for solutions, the problem was resolved. Children can be extremely good at finding pro-social solutions once the problem is clearly defined. The problem was the arguments; the solution was to agree a timetable for different children to have choices about what to watch. In this case it also involved recording some programmes for later viewing.

Sometimes restitution can be extended into positive practice so that the child has additional opportunities to learn what to do. For example, a child who occasionally wets his pants can be encouraged to practice going to the toilet a number of times so that he is reminded of what he needs to do to avoid accidents. As this becomes well-rehearsed it is more likely to occur next time it is needed.

Conclusion

This chapter has described some ways to manage problem behaviour that enable parents to plan in advance, let children know what the rules are, ensure that the opposite behaviour is being praised and rewarded and remain calm when dealing with problems. These ideas, along with those in the previous four chapters I have helped many parents to support their children's learning and to have happier and calmer homes.

7 Teaching new behaviour to our children

Many difficulties that parents have with children arise because they have not been taught more acceptable alternatives. So, teaching children alternative ways of behaving is important, and the previous chapters have already provided lots of examples about how to be an effective teacher. This chapter pulls together the ideas from the earlier chapters, particularly those on praise and rewards and on getting good at giving instructions (see Chapters 3 and 4). It starts by reminding us why focusing on problem behaviour can be counter-productive.

Children's views of themselves are strongly influenced by what has been said to them, and about them, by people around them. If children have been constantly told that they are naughty or bad or dishonest, they will come to see themselves in this way. This can have the effect of their continuing to behave in this way because that is the expectation that exists about them. This may have longer-term negative effects for children as they grow up, since many of the adults in our society who have mental health problems also have difficulty in interacting positively with other adults and have low self-esteem.

Sometimes we can deal with problem behaviour by using consequences (see Chapter 6). However, this needs to be done in a calm and planned manner or it may be achieved at a cost that parents would not wish to pay. We all learn by imitation and modelling, so if we are angry we might teach more by how we handle the situation than we do about the specific problem. For example, bigger or stronger or more powerful people (or even countries) influence the behaviour of the smaller and weaker people through aggression, nagging or verbal abuse. Unfortunately, the modelling principle tells us that children will then do the same in their own interactions with other people. Most bullies are children who have been treated in similar ways themselves.

Focusing on reducing problems can also lead to avoidance. A husband who was always met by his wife waiting to nag him when he got home from the pub took to staying out later and later each night. By doing this he avoided the nagging for as long as possible and sometimes his wife had gone to bed so he avoided it completely. In this case helping his wife to change her response when he came in led to a reversal in his pattern of drinking and staying out late. Clearly his wife's negative attention was not helping. Another similar result occurred for a child coming in from school and going to tell her Mum about what she has been doing in school that day. She was told that she had torn her trousers or got them dirty. This made it less likely that she would come to tell her Mum about what she had been doing in school. This was not what the parent intended any more than what the wife intended by nagging her husband when he came home. Another difficulty with focusing on problem behaviour is that it can teach children to lie in order to avoid consequences. Once lying becomes an established avoidance pattern it is difficult to stop doing it.

Frequently, parents complain that children do not tell them about things that they have been doing outside the home. Sometimes this is a situational problem, as reported by Suzy's mum. Asking how Suzy's day in school went is a very appropriate parent behaviour because taking an interest in a child's education is associated with good school outcomes for children, but you have to choose the right time. Imagine that you were five-year-old Suzy and had been in school all day. You come running out. You are met by a parent who asks you what you have done in school. But that is not what was on Suzy's mind because she was thinking about what she would do next, getting home, her favourite TV programme, etc. So she says "colouring". Mum then asks what she had for dinner and she says "Chips". These may be truthful answers but they are not very rewarding for her Mum who wants to learn about Suzy's day. So, seeing the world through Suzy's eyes helped Mum to solve this problem.

Here are the steps that led to a solution.

1. When greeting Suzy tell her that you have missed her and been thinking about her.
2. Ask Suzy what she wants to do when she gets home.

3. Talk to Suzy about what you had been doing during the day (modelling!).

4. Choose a quiet time to ask Suzy about school, for example at bed-time (a time when most children will talk to delay saying goodnight).

These four steps produced a surprising solution in that, once greeted and Mum having chatted a bit with Suzy, as they walked home together Suzy began to spontaneously tell her mother all about her school day.

Although sometimes necessary (see Chapter 6), having a strategy for dealing with problem behaviour is not a substitute for teaching children how we want them to behave. It is only when we focus on teaching something more appropriate that we are effective. In general it is better to spend more time focusing on what we want children to do and identifying strategies to teach these behaviours.

So, what are our teaching tools?

A. Reward behaviour we want to see more of

The first important teaching tool is to ensure that there are rewarding consequences. Here, we are talking mainly about our attention. Effective rewards have several important characteristics, particularly when we are concerned with teaching new behaviour, and these are described in Chapter 3, so are only summarised here.

1. Rewards should occur every time. We are often trying to establish habits, such as cleaning teeth, washing, etc. Once the behaviour occurs frequently it becomes part of a routine and the rewards need not, any longer, occur every time. Nevertheless, it is important, initially at least, to reward the behaviour every time since this is an important component of motivation to learn.

2. Rewards must be immediate if they are to become an effective part of teaching. We want to let children learn the relationship between their behaviour and our response as quickly as possible.

3. Rewards must also be effective. That means that we have to identify the rewards that are important for each child. Every child is different; most like praise but it may depend on how it is done.

A teenage son once told his Mum, "I'll tell you what I did in school mum as long as you don't 'reinforce' me". His Mum worked with severely learning disabled adults and was in the habit of giving effusive praise to any adaptive behaviour and for a teenager this was quite inappropriate.

B. Establish the Basic Skills for Learning

There are a number of skills that learners must have, including:

1. **Teach children to pay attention**
   This is a very important skill for a learner and, often, parents try to teach children without having established basic attention skills. Parents must teach a child to look at them, and this may mean removing the child from other distractions such as TV. There may be other good reasons for doing this as there is growing evidence of an association between the amount of time spent watching TV and problems such as ADHD. Getting children's attention can reduce the necessity to say things several times. Parents often repeat things to children and they may inadvertently have taught them that paying attention is unnecessary because the message will be repeated. Getting a child to repeat what has been said is one way of encouraging attention. Using a child's name to get their attention is also important. All of the other key principles in Chapter 4, on instruction following, also help.

Key Rules for supporting adolescents

1. Find time to be with them.
2. Praise them.
3. Positive attention.
4. Set achievable limits.
5. Let them bring friends home.
6. Be consistent
7. Ask them how

2. Imitation

Imitation is a major skill that we use to encourage learning and parents usually start to teach children to imitate when they are very young. We do this in several ways; one is by imitating what the child does – adults often repeat back the babbling noises that a young child makes. They also encourage children to imitate by waving to them and at the same time physically helping children to wave bye-bye, or blow kisses. As adults we are perhaps less dependent on imitation, except when we are in new situations and look to see what other people do. For example, when presented with food that we have not eaten before. Do other people eat it with a fork or a spoon? Do they eat the skin etc.? Sometimes, children have learned to imitate only the most inappropriate things that they hear or see, such as swearing, perhaps because this leads to a lot of attention, whereas more adaptive imitation may escape a parent's notice so it is not repeated. However it is important to recognise that imitation only works if the child is rewarded for repeating the behaviour that they have seen.

Methods of teaching

1. **Prompting the behaviour we want**

   We can prompt behaviour in a variety of ways. Once the behaviour is established the prompts can be faded out. In teaching toileting, as an example, we can start by prompting children to use the toilet by telling them when to go. We might do this because we are going to take them out and want to avoid an accident or because we notice some of the cues that suggest that they have a full bladder, such as crossing their legs or increased fidgeting. Sometimes we prompt children physically by sitting them on the potty or taking them to the toilet. Physical prompting can help to teach many other sorts of skills, for example, feeding. We might put our hand over the child's hand to guide it through the necessary action.

   Often, once going to the toilet is becoming established, we shift our prompts to asking questions of the child such as, "Do you want to go to the toilet?" This helps to start shifting the responsibility

for deciding what to do over to the child. This can help too in trying to teach social behaviour to children; for example, by asking a child "What would be a friendly way to ask your brother to share his toys?"

Once the child has started to learn we can start to fade our prompts. The child who initially went to the toilet because he was prompted by his parents soon started to go when he identified the signal that his bladder was full.

2. **Modelling**

Sometimes we can help children to learn by modelling, particularly if we have already taught them to imitate. The mother of a learning disabled boy was anxious because he always sat down on the

toilet even though she asked him to stand. Because he needed help to undress, his mother always took him into the ladies toilets with her. He was not good at understanding and following verbal instructions and he had not learned to stand up to pass urine. Once his father took responsibility for teaching him, and demonstrated what to do, he quickly learned.

3. **Making sure our goals are achievable – identifying realistic teaching steps**

   Most of the things that we try to teach children are quite complex and involve several steps, so it is not surprising that they sometimes have difficulty in learning. This is apparent, even with independent toileting, which is successfully acquired by the average two-year-old. To be "independent" in toileting children must recognise bladder and bowel cues, must know where the toilet is, probably be able to open doors, undress and dress themselves, climb on to the seat, etc. Often children's failure to learn is a consequence of failure on the part of the parent to analyse the task and to teach all the necessary skills. When a more detailed analysis is made, a more realistic teaching target can be established, probably leading towards independent toileting, which becomes a longer-term goal. Analysis of the components of the task can also be done for the individual skills involved, such as dressing, and smaller goals can often be set such as pulling pants up and down.

4. **Teaching the last bit of the task first**
    Starting by asking them to do the last bit of the task can be a useful way to help children to learn. For example, putting on socks is a complex chain of behaviours and it is not surprising that some young children get frustrated and tell their parents that they can't do it. Rather than doing it for them, parents can start by putting the child's sock almost on and over the heel and asking the child just to pull it up for the last two inches. The child can soon learn to do this and will be encouraged by this success to attempt more of the task. This can also be a successful way of teaching children to do jig saw puzzles, initially getting them to put just the last piece in, then the last two pieces, etc. The advantage of this strategy is that as you teach the next part of the task it always leads on to the part that they have already mastered.

5. **Shaping**

   Another helpful teaching strategy is to gradually increase the performance that is required. This is particularly the case when we are teaching language. At first the child's approximation to a new word is acceptable to the parents. "Bish" was initially sufficient to send a parent of an 18 month old searching for a book, with a fish on the cover. When the parents subsequently demanded more it was improved to "pish", which at first was accepted because the "p" sound was a more complex one which the child had not used before. When subsequently, the child was prompted to say "fish" this was soon mastered. This shaping process operates in the way that we teach many skills. It helped in teaching a child to play the recorder. Initially, the parent praised the child because the correct fingers were in place although the notes did not always sound correct. Next, the child was encouraged to listen to the sound and make sure that the holes were properly covered to ensure that the notes sounded right as well.

Conclusion

In general, successful teaching depends on a number of specific skills. These include:

1. Identifying the alternative behaviour required by children rather than punishing inappropriate behaviour.
2. Identifying the necessary skills required by the child to achieve the target behaviour.

3. Finding ways of breaking teaching tasks into components that the child can achieve.
4. Working out the best teaching strategies in the form of prompting, shaping and modelling.
5. Rewarding the child for success.

Using these teaching skills will ensure that children are supported in being successful learners.

8 Developing children's language

Understanding and using language is an important human skill, probably our most complex skill. Every society has language and many things are taught through language, including our cultural history and values. Culture is our accumulated knowledge, wisdom, beliefs and language allows us to transmit experiences and knowledge, both across and within generations without the necessity of direct experience. It is also involved in thinking, memory, reasoning, problem-solving, perception and managing our emotions. It is clear from the earlier chapters how important language is in terms of listening to our children, giving specific labelled praise, giving clear instructions, labelling emotions and social skills and giving clear explanations of consequences.

Helping children's language development is important to facilitate their understanding of the meaning of other people's words (comprehension), to help them to express themselves (communication), to help them to understand and manage their own behaviour (self-control) and to understand that of others (empathy). Although our brains are programmed to acquire it, the actual language we develop is learned, children acquire

the language or languages that they hear. This is so obvious that it is almost trivial to say, we do not expect a child who grows up exposed to French to speak Welsh, but we sometimes forget how important we are as children's language teachers.

The principles described in this book are important in encouraging language acquisition. In particular, shaping, prompting, imitation, praise and rewards all play an important part. When we consider what a complicated skill language is, it is remarkable that most children speak fluently by the age of four. This is when the tantrums of two and three-year-olds start to be replaced, for most children, by an understanding of what they can have and what is expected of them. As a result, their growing ability to understand rules about what is required of them and why, helps them to fit in with the world around them.

Imitation

By nine or ten months parents have taught most children to imitate waving bye-bye, pat-a-cake games, etc. At the same time parents often imitate their children's babble, which often has the effect of setting up a series of inter-actions such as: child makes sound "bo"; mum repeats sound "bo"; the child continues to make the sound "bo"; mum repeats again. In this way the mother is teaching the child to imitate by first imitating the child and making it much more likely that the child will imitate her. Most parents, often quite unknowingly, model behaviour for children, for example, when a parent is feeding a very young child they often open their own mouth as they take the spoon towards the child's mouth.

Shaping and prompting

During their first six months, most babies produce the sounds that appear in all languages including guttural, trills and other complex and quite specific sounds. It can be difficult to differentiate the early babbling of the baby of one society from that of another, but by about nine or ten months the range of babbled sounds narrows.

Whilst initially paying attention to every sound, parents gradually start to provide more attention to sounds that are more typical of their own language or are progressively closer approximations to particular words; thus "da" may be reinforced as an approximation to "daddy", "mmm ..." for "mummy" or later "dink" for "drink". Gradually the child learns to produce something that is closer to the actual word expected. When a child of 18 months holds out a hand towards a biscuit and maybe also says "ta" this might be accepted. Parents generally respond by saying "so you want a biscuit", so at first they are expanding on what the child has said without expecting the child to say it. Gradually parents require the child to extend the statement by asking them to say "biscuit please", making their request more accurate.

After learning single words, children soon start to develop skills in using word combinations, and, when they are very young, parents focus on the meaning of children's language rather than correct grammar. This is not surprising because parents are trying to understand what the child is trying to communicate. A psychologist called Brown described how the parent of a young girl, Eve, responded to her saying, "He a girl", by answering "That's right". Similarly, "Her curl my hair", was approved because the mother was in fact curling Eve's hair. However, Sarah's grammatically correct "There's the animal farmhouse", was corrected because the building was a lighthouse and Adam's "Walt Disney comes on Tuesday", was corrected because Walt Disney came on another day. These examples of shaping language development show how the focus on meaning comes before grammar. This demonstrates how parents understand how important it is to understand children's communication efforts and realise that they can teach them grammatical rules later.

By the age of one the average child moves from babbling to whole words, which usually represent objects. By 18 months the words can stand for whole sentences; for example, holding out a hand and saying "ball" is a request for a ball. Learning any task usually starts slowly and then rapidly speeds up, and language is a particularly good example. Children have an average of four words at age one, 200 words at age 2, 800 words at age 3 and 2,000 at age 4. Learning to recognise and use one word from the very complex language of the world around you is a much bigger task than adding another word to those that you already know. The more words that the child has, the easier it is to spot the pattern and meaning of a new one.

For very young children, speech is a means of communication with adults and other children. Subsequently, it also becomes a means whereby children organise their experiences and regulate their own actions and young children often give themselves instructions out loud. As children mature, talking to themselves becomes an ever more powerful influence over their own behaviour and they shift from spoken to silent speech in their head (thinking), which helps them to learn other complex skills.

The way that we understand the world depends on the language that we have developed to organise our perception. Different cultures label things more precisely when they have significance for that society. The range of words in Arabic to describe sand and in Inuit to describe snow are functions of the greater importance that these things have in the lives of their people, and these different labels allow clearer descriptions of the situation.

Some years ago, Basil Bernstein, a sociologist, became interested in language and looked at what he called restricted and elaborated language. He found that some parents tended to use short, simple, grammatically uncomplicated and easily understood sentences, primarily denoting things and actions; whereas others emphasised the use of language in socialising and disciplining their children, teaching them moral standards and communicating feelings and emotions. Since we now know the importance of helping children to use

language to interpret feelings and to manage their own behaviour, it is clear that it is important to encourage children's language skills in all of these spheres.

Children's self-esteem is closely tied to the messages that people around them have given them about themselves, so wrapping children in positive language is an important skill. All of this helps us to understand why it is important that children are encouraged to have the best possible opportunity to learn their first language, or languages, so that they can understand what others say, communicate what they are feeling and manage their own behaviour. To encourage this parents need to:

1. **Talk to children whenever possible**
   Make sure that you are describing what you are doing and what your child is doing whenever possible. This helps to develop children's vocabulary and also, as a by-product, strengthens your relationship with them by showing your interest in their activities.

2. **Use words that label feelings**
   It is important that children have words for feelings, since this will give them opportunities to think about and decide what to do and how to handle their feelings. A lot of feelings that we will label will be positive ones. We can label our own feelings: "I am happy when I see you playing nicely with your brother". You can also label your child's feelings; "you look happy", "you must be

feeling proud of yourself". It is also important to give children labels for feelings that are uncomfortable: "You must have felt disappointed when ..." "I can see that you are frustrated because your tower fell down"; giving these words for feelings helps children to understand, manage and talk about their own feelings.

3. **Teach self-calming talk**

    It is important to label things like staying calm in a situation where the child is angry or frustrated. Using words like: "it is not easy but you are having another go", "trying again" or "sticking at it", will also help children to manage situations where things are not working out as they would like.

4. **Teach children to reflect and problem solve**

    Using language that helps children to think about how to solve problems is helpful. After all, one day they will leave home and have to find their own solutions, so it is never too early to start. This can be a two-way process; it can involve prompting children to think of solutions, "I wonder what you could do to make the tower stand up"; or it could use various forms of prompting such as "maybe if you turned the block around the other way" or "maybe a different piece fits there".

5. **Teach children to give compliments by praising them**

    Giving compliments or saying friendly things to other people is an important social skill and, in fact, the most popular children are the ones who say friendly things to other children. So, we really want to encourage children to do this. The two teaching skills of modelling, through the compliments that we give to our children, and prompting by saying to one child: "don't you think that your brother did a good job, what could you say to him?" are great ways to do this.

Conclusion

Language competence depends on the way in which it is taught and all of the principles for teaching new behaviour are relevant to language learning. Sometimes problem behaviour happens because, although children's demands are not inappropriate, the method of making the demand is. It may involve teaching children to ask politely for a biscuit rather than having a tantrum. It is important to find ways of continuing to develop children's language throughout childhood, so as to enable them to increasingly be able to express emotions and understand and recognise the needs of others. Parents should prioritise the development of these essential skills in their children to aid their understanding, communication, self-regulation and empathy for others.

9 Summing it all up

Behavioural challenges are common among young children, with phrases like the "terrible twos" or "tantrumming three-year-olds" often heard. It is generally because children's independence can run ahead of their comprehension at that age. However, for some children these problems persist. This book has described a toolkit of the most important things that parents can do to support their children's development. These are useful, both for parents facing everyday challenges and for parents with children with developmental or other difficulties that persist across children's early years.

We started by emphasising the importance of letting children know that they are important to us. Whilst we might be concerned to help children to follow instructions, we need to recognise that they are much more likely to do this for someone who appreciates and understands them. So, the ideas about ways of building and strengthening our relationship with our children are most important, not only for children's self-esteem, but also because they will encourage our children to cooperate with us.

Having established a firm base to our relationship with our children we are then in the position to encourage, or strengthen, the things we would like our children to do more of. Chapter 3 describes how to make our praise effective and specific so that children clearly understand what behaviour we would like to see more of and how to provide small rewards.

Chapter 4 describes ways of becoming more effective in helping children to follow instructions. The core principle that children need four times more attention for positive behaviour than they do for problem behaviour applies to this and the following chapters.

The combination of Chapters 2–4, building relationships, praising and rewarding, and giving clear instructions are the foundations upon which effective ignoring and limit setting (Chapters 5 and 6) will work.

Chapter 5 describes key principles for ignoring. Parents can find it hard to learn to ignore effectively, however, as long as children are generally in the "sunshine of positive attention", ignoring is a powerful tool.

Chapter 6 describes ways for dealing with problem behaviour or serious rule infringements such as aggression. The most important thing to remember here is the four to one rule; that whatever problem behaviour we deal with must be addressed in the context of a situation where children have many more opportunities to receive positive attention for their behaviour. The other key rule is to be consistent.

Chapter 7 summarises ways to teach new behaviours to children. This is really important since we cannot reliably remove problem behaviour (we may find that we have a different problem behaviour), so it is important to teach children positive ways of behaving that are rewarded.

Chapter 8 reminds us of the importance of wrapping children in language. This includes describing what children are doing, labelling feelings, both our own and those that children may be experiencing, as well as all of the other key ideas about being specific in our praise and clear in our instructions.

The ideas in this book are not new and have helped many parents. They have come from many years of support for parents and children both from my own work and that of many colleagues.

The key principle that we must always remember is that "we are models for our children's behaviour". Our children learn an enormous amount from the way that we behave towards them, how we communicate with them and how we let them know that we are there to support them. Children need to live in "the sunshine of positive attention".

10 Typical problems experienced by real families
Positive parenting in action

Solving a bedtime problem

Consequences significantly influence how we learn and whether things will happen again. So, it is important to look first at why they are happening. Night-time problems are common and, by considering what consequences there might be, we can find solutions for these problems for many children. This is important because there is growing evidence to the extent to which the behaviour of both children and adults in our society is affected by sleep deprivation, highlighting the importance of good sleep routines.

Andrew was three-years-old and his night-time behaviour was a major problem for his parents. His daytime behaviour was also challenging and he was described as hyperactive. However, his parents saw the night-time problem as imposing the most limitations on them as a family. If Andrew did not have a lot of attention at night he made his parents' life a misery. He would not go to bed when asked, if they did get him into bed he would not remain there on his own and although he lived in a three-bedroom house his bed was in his parents' bedroom, although generally he ended up sleeping in their bed.

At bedtime, usually at the fourth or fifth time of asking, he would go upstairs to his bedroom with one of his parents. Once in bed he would demand a drink and snack, and his parent would go downstairs to get this for him and then, after stories, they would stay with him until he fell asleep. This could last for well over an hour. Once he was asleep, they would creep downstairs only to find that, at least five times a week, Andrew would wake up and either call for someone to come upstairs or come downstairs himself. Generally, he came downstairs and then remained downstairs until they all went to bed. If he remained asleep until after his parents had gone to bed he then got into their bed when he woke up, so he ended up in their bed every morning. Whilst downstairs, he sat or lay on the settee between his parents – he would not let them sit together. Finally, all three went to bed together and Andrew slept between his parents in their bed for the rest of the night. Andrew's younger sister did not have these problems, but she was still in a cot so, as yet, she did not have a choice about getting up.

When Andrew was three and a half his parents asked for help. Tranquillisers had already been tried without much effect so their doctor referred them for help with his management. By now the night-time problems had been occurring for over two and a half years and were affecting many other aspects of family life. His parents said that the hyperactive and challenging day time behaviour had developed more recently. Andrew's parents could not get a babysitter so they could not go out together and had little privacy. They disagreed about the best way to solve the problem and blamed each other for the situation. They said that they had tried everything, including threats, bribes and punishment.

It was easy to see why Andrew continued to behave in this way. There were many rewards for him. He got attention from his parents as well as drinks and food through the night. But how had he learned it?

When Andrew was born his parents had lived in a one-bedroom flat so he had always slept in the same room with them. When he was 10 months old he had been quite ill and had several disturbed nights. His parents had got up when he cried to see what was wrong and soothed him back to sleep. This led to demands for attention at night that gradually increased in frequency. By the time Andrew's parents began to realise that he was not in pain there was a well-established pattern that they had since not managed to change.

There were several reasons for Andrew's parents failing to get to grips with the problem. His Mum said:

> Well, we have tried putting him back in his own bed but he makes such a fuss and cries. That disturbs my husband and he has to get his sleep just now because he's hoping for promotion and he's being watched at work to see whether they think he could do it.

In fact Andrew's Dad sometimes slept in a separate bedroom. So a further issue was their concern that he would wake his sister.

Andrew's problem was typical of that reported by many parents and there is usually a logical explanation for how the behaviour became established, in Andrew's case, during illness, or following a period in hospital. By the time the problem was established Andrew had learned the rewarding consequences of his behaviour and his parents had learned that, in the short term, giving in was the least painful way to cope.

Andrew's parents agreed to a plan to teach him more acceptable ways of behaving at bedtime and during the night. First, they kept simple records of what was happening before trying to change things. These included recording what time Andrew went to bed, how long they laid with him, whether he had drinks or food in bed, what time he got up, also whether he spent the night in his parents' bed. Andrew's parents kept records over eight nights which showed that they were lying with him for, on average, 47 minutes each night before he fell asleep. He later spent every one of the eight nights in his parents' bed. Andrew's parents could see that there were many rewarding consequences for him which were maintaining his difficult behaviour and a new routine was devised:

1. Tell Andrew that you have a new plan for him to earn stickers for sleeping in his own bed each night.
2. Tell Andrew that he can have food or drinks in the kitchen before going to bed. Andrew was a fussy daytime eater – not surprising when he had food during the night, including quite a lot of milk that substitutes for food!

3. Going to bed: take Andrew to bed and read stories for 10 minutes. Tell him that he is a big boy now and that he is learning to stay in his own bed. Explain to him that if he shouts after you have gone downstairs you will not reply. Remind him that if he comes downstairs he will be taken back to bed.

4. Tell Andrew that he can tell his grandmother all about learning to sleep on his own. Andrew was very fond of his grandmother and also liked to speak on the phone.

5. In the evening if Andrew comes downstairs take him back to bed without speaking to him. The same applies if he comes to your bed during the night when you are in bed. You may, at first, have to do this a lot of times. He must end the night sleeping in his own bed.

6. In the morning remind Andrew that he is a big boy and that he has stayed in his own bed all night and give him a sticker to put on his chart. Make it very clear how pleased you are that he is in his own bed regardless of how many times you have had to put him back in his own bed.

7. During the day remind Andrew, at first several times, that he stayed in his own bed during the night and also tell any other visitors to the house or anyone that you see with Andrew about his good behaviour. Let Andrew speak to his grandmother on the phone to tell her he stayed in his own bed.

The plan was discussed in detail before commencement and Andrew's parents were prepared for the fact that Andrew's initial response would probably be challenging. They were however, reassured that if they were consistent this plan was likely to produce observable changes within less than a week. It was also important to establish that they would support one another in carrying out the plan to put Andrew back to bed without getting angry with him. This involved coaching them in some positive self-talk about the benefits for Andrew as well as for themselves. On the first night Andrew came downstairs 47 times but he learned to sleep in his own bed very quickly. On the second night he came down once. He did not come downstairs again after being put to bed until the 10th night, when he again tried once.

This was a clear demonstration to Andrew's parents of how children's behaviour will change, usually quite quickly, sometimes very dramatically, when the consequences change. Under the new system the rewards for staying in his own bed, and the removal of the rewarding consequences previously associated with the problem, rapidly taught Andrew to do this.

Within less than a month Andrew was sleeping in a room on his own all night. His parents had felt that moving him out of their bedroom was too large a step for Andrew, so they decided to move themselves into a slightly smaller bedroom that they had previously intended for Andrew, leaving him in the room that he was familiar with. They also did a great job in rearranging the consequences for his behaviour using a combination of giving positive attention for the behaviour they wanted, with reinforcement for target behaviour, and ignoring the behaviour that they wanted less of. They also said that having the plan meant that they handled the situation much more calmly than they had previously done, thereby modelling positive behaviour towards Andrew. Having a very structured plan made it possible for Andrew's parents to approach the situation calmly and explain to Andrew in advance what the new system involved and what the rewards for Andrew would be.

Another benefit was a significant improvement in Andrew's daytime behaviour, something that can occur quite often. Recent studies suggest that children, adolescents and adults are getting insufficient sleep, and that this can have a major impact on daytime levels of concentration.

It is important to establish what is reinforcing the night-time problem, which is usually clearly demonstrated if parents keep record sheets. The child may obtain access to food and drinks or TV or toys in the bedroom, or the problem may be anxiety based and the parent remaining with the child might reduce the child's anxiety. Some children are afraid of the dark, usually ones that have not experienced it and strategies such as installing dimmer lights or sitting with the child in the bedroom in the dark may be needed to help children learn to feel comfortable in the dark. Light of any sort in the bedroom reduces the production of melatonin during sleep and this can disrupt sleep rhythms and the body's care and repair mechanisms. Some children may be ill-prepared for sleep due to being overstimulated as a result of too much time in front of screens, particularly if the content includes violent games. Many studies have confirmed the effects of exposure to violent media, particularly on younger children and on boys. Current advice suggests the need for two screen-free hours prior to going to bed in order that the brain is prepared for sleep.

Key points that led to success in the work with Andrew were:

1. A clear description of the problem to enable the identification of probable reinforcers or rewards.
2. This information helped Andrew's parents to work out a plan.
3. The plan was introduced to Andrew in a positive way.
4. Andrew's parents knew what challenges would be faced in implementing the plan, e.g. that on the first night Andrew was likely to get out of bed many times.
5. Andrew's parents talked through how they would support one another in ensuring that they stayed calm and stuck to the plan.

For this, and many other problems, it can be helpful to introduce the new plan in stages, such as first establishing the rule that food is only eaten in a certain place or getting a structured bedtime routine in place before addressing the larger aspect of the problem or only returning a child to their own bed if they wake during the night. In Andrew's case he was developmentally capable of learning the new behaviour if his parents implemented the whole plan at once. The fact that both of his parents were willing to support each other in doing this also contributed to their decision to address the problem in this way.

A morning problem

In the previous example changing the consequences helped Andrew to learn to stay in bed at night. In this example a similar approach was used to address a morning problem.

Steven was 11 and had difficulty getting up in the morning and it was getting worse. First his Dad woke him. Then, on her way downstairs, his Mum said good morning to him and asked him to get up. She started to prepare the breakfast and, if she could not hear Steven moving, she would go to the foot of the stairs and call him, often several times. The calls would escalate to shouts and, since this seldom worked, she often had to go upstairs and actually shake him out of bed. When he finally arrived in the kitchen Stephen usually got a telling off for his disobedience and for making himself late for school.

For Steven, there were not many pleasant consequences associated with mornings. His Mum nagged him and shouted at him, not only when he remained upstairs, but also when he came down. But the consequence for Steven's Mum was that the end result of all her nagging was that Steven finally got up – so she continued to do it day after day, not very happy, but trapped by a situation in which nagging and shouting seemed to be the only thing that worked. She had inadvertently taught Steven that she took the responsibility for getting him up and, in order to achieve this, she had to do a lot of nagging and shouting.

Steven's Mum knew that something needed to change and keeping records of what was happening helped her to identify the problem more clearly and rearrange the consequences to teach Steven to get up more readily. Given Steven's age it was important to include him in the discussion of both the problem and the plan. First Mum clearly identified what Steven needed to do in the morning. He must get out of bed, wash his hands and face, get dressed and come downstairs. His Mum put out his morning clothes on the previous evening. Steven agreed that it should be possible to do this in 25 minutes and he readily agreed with his parents that if he did achieve 25 minutes or less he could have an extra half hour of television time in the evening. Steven's Mum agreed to only ask Steven once to get up and not to call or nag him. She also agreed to smile and say something pleasant when he came down, regardless of how long he had taken in getting up.

Sometimes when working on strategies to solve problems like this it can be helpful if parents inform schools or employers that the child might be late for school for a day or two or the parent late for work. However, most children do not like being late for school and helping them to take responsibility for their own behaviour is usually a very powerful tool in helping them to change.

On day one, following the usual routine, first Steven's Dad woke him, then his Mum said good morning to him and asked him to get up on her way downstairs. Steven took 55 minutes to get downstairs. It was difficult for his mother to refrain from doing what she had previously done but once Steven came downstairs she smiled and said, "Nice to see you" and then later said, "I am sorry to say that you have not earned your half hour of extra TV time tonight. I think that tomorrow you will manage to do it". By expressing her sympathy for Steven's failure to earn the reward his Mum was modelling her own concern for him and her wish for him to succeed. This was a different response to that which his behaviour had previously generated, which tended to be anger.

On day two Steven took 26 minutes to get downstairs and his Mum greeted him cheerfully and acknowledged that he had been quicker but repeated what she had said the previous day. She almost relented since it was so close, but she reasoned that 26 minutes today would be 27 minutes tomorrow, and so on. Thereafter, Steven was down well inside the 25 minutes and earned his extra TV time. Within a couple of weeks they had stopped timing him or mentioning the routine but continued to praise him on arrival downstairs. As well as gaining the extra

TV time, both Steven and his Mum were rewarded for their new behaviour by pleasant mornings.

In this situation the behaviour that had achieved consequences for Mum, nagging and shouting, had continued however unpleasant she found it, because it worked and she did not know how else to get Steven to get up. For Steven the consequence of getting up was a further telling off so was delayed as long as possible. Mum had taken on the responsibility for getting him up and Steven had learned to ignore what she said for as long as possible.

It is important to ensure that the behaviour you want has happened, and in Steven's case his Mum was certain that he did wash his hands and face and that this did not need supervising.

However, for some children a much greater level of supervision is needed to ensure that the behaviour occurs and that each step can be praised and rewarded. It is not uncommon for parents and children to argue about whether the child has done something, such as their homework or cleaning their teeth.

Many parents find themselves in the same situation as Steven's mum, knowing very clearly what they want their child to do but having got into a trap of providing consequences for the wrong behaviour and/or having failed to set up consequences for the right behaviour. Solutions generally require the following steps (a) careful observation of what is currently happening, to identify what consequences are currently operating; (b) deciding what the desired behaviour is and that it is developmentally achievable; (c) ensuring that rewarding consequences are arranged for the appropriate behaviour rather than for anything else.

We can learn a lot about consequences from the examples of Steven and Andrew. Two sorts of consequences encourage behaviour to occur again. Behaviour is repeated when something pleasant follows. Steven soon learnt to get up quickly on his own because he got more TV and his Mum was nice to him. Andrew stayed in bed at night because he got praise and attention for it. Behaviour is also repeated when what we do removes something unpleasant. Andrew's parents gave in to his demands at bedtime and during the night because it was an end to the difficulties presented if they tried to manage the situation in any other way. Before Steven had learned to get up through his own efforts he got up only when the nagging and shouting became so unpleasant that it was impossible to stay in bed any longer. Getting up put an end to this unpleasant nagging.

The key message from these examples is to give attention to behaviour we want more of and remove attention from behaviour we want less of. It is also important to remember that parents are models for their children and that children learn as much from the way that parents handle situations (in this case calmly and pleasantly rather than by nagging) as they do about the situations themselves.

In learning to recognise and change the consequences of problem behaviour, it can be helpful to keep records of the problem and what follows it. Record keeping sometimes resolves problems because it shows parents what is happening and what needs changing. In some cases, writing down what is happening when a problem occurs changes how parents respond to it (they become detectives looking for clues to explain behaviour and so respond differently to it) and this too can produce changes in children's behaviour.

In the 1970s an Australian psychologist did a study that involved getting parents to record typical things that their child did that they found problematic. She developed lists of typical behaviours for children of different ages. For three-year-olds it included tantrums, hitting, spitting, swearing, running off, throwing objects, etc. Parents were asked to keep the list on their fridge or cupboard door and go to the list whenever the problem behaviour occurred and to mark it down and say to themselves: "This is what three-year-olds do". She found that the act of walking away and recording the problem actually reduced it. This was because the behaviour no longer got the attention that it previously had. It also served to help the parents to recognise that these problems were typical of children at that age, so provided developmental knowledge that helped parents to have more realistic expectations.

Two things are important to consider in the case of Stephen. He was expected to undertake, getting up washing dressing etc. before coming downstairs and without supervision. In his case he was already doing all of these things without supervision so the task was developmentally achievable and did not need teaching. The only teaching that was needed was for Stephen to respond to the initial prompt. For many children more supervision would be needed and the programme might need to focus on one step at a time and may need teaching and/or supervision. In addressing a morning problem it would also be important to consider whether the child had an adequate amount of sleep or whether tiredness was playing a part in the problem as discussed in the bed-time example earlier.

A shopping trip

A common problem for parents can be seen at the till in the supermarket. Some mothers with young children may try to leave them at home when they go shopping and some cope well in the supermarket, but for some being confronted by tiers of sweets at the till can be a challenge where you might overhear the following:

Child: "Can I have ...?"
Mum: "No!"

Child starts to repeat more loudly "Can I have?" or cry –

Mum says "No" rather more loudly.

The child tries to grab the sweets or to tantrum – Mum tries to maintain her position.

Other people start to take notice.

Mum picks up the sweets and puts them into the shopping trolley.

Child beams and peace is restored.

Two things have been rewarded. First the child was rewarded for shouting and getting sweets by the tantrum, therefore, he or she will do it again. Secondly, the mother was rewarded for giving in to the child's difficult behaviour because the child becomes quiet and other customers stop taking notice of what is happening. She too is likely to cope in the same way next time. This is the same pattern as we saw with Andrew's night-time problem. The child's behaviour is rewarded by the positive consequence. In this case the sweets and the mother is rewarded because the child stops behaving badly and the problem goes away.

What has happened makes sense in terms of consequences for both the child and the parent. The problem that it produces is a longer-term one, reminding us that behaviour that is reinforced will be repeated.

Sometimes the consequence of, or reward for, problem behaviour is attention, but often, it involves other things: sweets, extra computer time, staying up later to watch TV, etc. By identifying and removing the rewards for problem behaviour, and by ensuring that they only follow desired behaviour, problems can be resolved without having to resort to punishment, as was demonstrated in the solution to the morning and night-time problems.

The till in the supermarket illustrates something else. People, even children, are very good at learning what will pay off in different situations and with different people, so it is important to look for the triggers, what prompts them to behave in a particular way at that time. These antecedents or triggers (the things that occur before the problem behaviour) can set off particular chains of events.

At the till in the supermarket there are several very important antecedents or triggers for problem behaviour. One is that people often have to wait, so children have nothing to do. Another is that the supermarket managers and owners, who also understand human psychology, put an array of easily available goods, often in reach of children, intended to prompt people to spend more money while they wait. Another antecedent, or trigger, is that there are usually other people standing around who might take notice. All of these things combine to make something much more likely to happen than others. So, looking at Antecedents (or triggers), Behaviour and Consequences – known as the ABC model – is very helpful in sorting out what is happening.

In the supermarket the situation looks a bit like the chart on the following page:

Linda was three and a half years old and had a younger sister of one and a half. Linda would touch things in

Antecedent for the child	Child's Behaviour	Consequences
Nothing to do, sitting in trolley by the till	Ask for sweets	Mum says no
Sweets within reach	Ask again louder	Mum says no
Other people join the queue	Start crying	Mum says no
People start to pay attention	Child tries to grab the sweets	Mum is embarrassed and says OK
Mum gives sweets to child	Child has the sweets	People stop paying attention
	Child no longer crying	Mum feels more comfortable

shops, pick them up and demand, successfully, that Mum bought her sweets. Her mother had got so upset about taking her shopping that she tried to do all her shopping in the two mornings that Linda was in the playgroup for a couple of hours. Mum also had difficulties in getting Linda to follow instructions at home.

Before Linda's Mum started taking her shopping again, she first helped Linda to follow instructions at home, but once this was done she tried the following:

1. Mum got Linda a small bag so that she could be like Mum and carry something home.
2. Mum told Linda that she would like her to hold the side of the trolley walking round the shop, but when Mum wanted something Linda could fetch it and put it in the trolley.

3. Mum told Linda that if she helped in the shop she would be able to choose something for herself to take home in her bag (since Linda was already being bought something when she went shopping her Mum decided that it was important that Linda got something for acceptable rather than for unacceptable behaviour).

4. If there were choices about things that Mum was buying, for instance, which sort of biscuits, Mum was asked to involve Linda in the choice.

5. Mum talked to Linda to retain her interest while shopping by telling her what they were going to buy, what meals they could make with it, and so on, and by asking Linda to remind her to get things. For an older child writing and carrying the shopping list and searching for things can be helpful.

6. Whilst in the shop Mum praised Linda and reminded her what a good girl she was for helping with the shopping and how nice it was to have such a good helper.

Initially Mum took Linda for very short shopping expeditions and into smaller shops, in fact first to the local village post-office where Linda was able to post a letter in the post box. Gradually, as Mum learned how to keep Linda's interest and teach her to help, she was able to extend the length of time and the locations in which she could shop with Linda without having problems. On the first few occasions Linda's Mum also took along a set of reins, which she explained before leaving home to Linda that she would have to put on if Linda wandered off in the way she previously had.

If we look at Linda's behaviour in ABC terms we can see what has happened.

Antecedent for problem	Behaviour	Consequences
Shops	Walk around, touch things, pick things up	Mums attention put that down, etc.
Seeing other people pick things up generally, including Mum, and seeing sweets at the till	Demand sweets	Sweets

Antecedent for solution	Behaviour	Consequences
Shops	Linda helps Mum	Mum praises her
Mum involves Linda in shopping	Linda helps with the shopping	Linda chooses something for herself

Other useful strategies for solving shopping problems include getting the child to help to write the shopping list, cutting out parts of cereal boxes etc. for the child to look for them and giving the child a sticker at the end of each shopping aisle for holding onto the trolley, helping to push it etc. The stickers can earn the small reward that the child will be able to choose something costing less than a pound.

The antecedents or triggers that produce problem behaviour can be a particular person previously associated with that behaviour when it has been rewarded. Granny, for example, might say yes to requests for sweets or ice creams more often than other people. Granny's arrival might become a trigger for asking for sweets. Children learn that there are times when parents will say yes and times when they will say no. They may say yes in the supermarket and no at home so the trigger for the problem is a particular place, such as school or a shop, or frustration because someone called you a name or took your toy. Being tired or hungry can also be a trigger for a particular behaviour or when a parent is otherwise occupied, on the phone or talking with a friend.

All of these examples show the importance of observing and describing very carefully not only the child's behaviour and the consequence but also the situation in which the behaviour occurs. Describing the situation means looking at where it is, who is present, what people were doing, and so on. Only by careful observation of this sort can we understand children's behaviour sufficiently to be able to help them learn what we want them to do.

A toileting problem

The problems described earlier, going to bed, getting up, and going shopping, were resolved by understanding how the situation was rewarding to both the child and the parent. They also showed how teaching the desired behaviour and providing consequences for it was effective in replacing problem behaviour with pro-social behaviour. Sometimes, what was rewarding the problem behaviour can be used as a reward for the new behaviour. For example, an older child who delays going to bed could earn half an hour of extra time out of bed for going to bed on time on school nights, which could be spent by staying up at weekends. This would only work with an older child as developmentally younger children are not yet likely to have learned to wait and would need a more immediate reward. The shopping problem involved helping Linda to earn the reward for acceptable behaviour rather than problem behaviour. The shopping trip also highlighted the importance of looking for triggers or antecedents, the situations that set up or prompt behaviour.

It is often easier to understand the effect of triggers for, or antecedents of, behaviour by looking at learning failures rather than successes. For example, a mother was giving her three-year-old son Peter lots of attention for sitting on the potty – so why wasn't he learning to use it? Her description of what was happening was:

> I notice that his pants are damp so I sit him on the potty and give him lots of attention. I make sitting on the potty pleasant, I read books to him while he sits there, and so on, but he does not do anything in it.

A more careful description of the problem revealed the following:

Antecedent	Behaviour	Consequences
Bladders signal indicating that Peter must empty his bladder	Peter wets his pants	Mum sits Peter on potty and gives lots of attention, reads to him, etc.

Peter was sat on the potty and given attention when he was wet and not when he was dry. He learned to use the potty within a week when his Mum changed the consequences.

Peter's Mum started to check his pants at frequent intervals, initially every 15 minutes. If Peter had wet pants he was changed without comment and not sat on the potty. If he was dry she praised him and also asked him: "Do you want a wee?" If he said yes he was praised and encouraged to sit on the potty where he was praised for a good decision but was not read to. If he said no he did not want a wee he was praised for being dry. If he used the potty, which she checked frequently, he was praised again. If, after 5 minutes on the potty, he had not performed he was praised for remaining dry and told that he could try again when he was ready. This simple change was sufficient to teach Peter to use the potty very quickly.

For Peter, being dry led to a consequence of praise, being wet led to being changed without anything being said. Obviously, since he became dry so quickly, the praise was a rewarding consequence. His Mum also continued to read frequently to Peter, something that is important for all children, but not when he was on the potty.

It is important that children are praised more for being dry than for performing, although it is sometimes helpful to prompt children, if we are going on a long journey for example. In general, we want children to learn to respond to a signal from their bladder that tells them that they need to go to the toilet. Both the presence of Mum and the bladder signals can be antecedents which lead to the behaviour we want, but it is only when the child learns to respond to bladder cues that they become independent in toileting. There is a maturational process underpinning bladder control and children are generally not ready to learn until they have developed control and have sufficient urine in their bladders to become aware of bladder cues. This can be judged by the frequency and amount of urine when the child does pass urine and that becomes more apparent with the dry pants checks. Had Peter's Mum found that his pants were wet very frequently she would have needed to consider whether he was developmentally capable of learning at that stage or whether he needed some other form of assessment.

Another example of the power of antecedents comes from another toileting problem. A social worker had worked with a mother on toilet training Tommy, a child with a significant developmental difficulty and had taken an active part in helping with his toilet-training. Unfortunately, the wrong message had been learned.

Tommy had learned to associate the social worker with sitting on the potty rather than to respond to bladder cues. Every time she arrived at the house Tommy rushed off and got his potty and sat on it. He usually managed to perform something and got her attention but was not responding to his bladder cues:

Antecedent	Behaviour	Consequences
Jane arrives	Tommy sits on potty passes a small amount of urine	Praise from Jane

This was easily resolved by the social worker shifting her attention from Tommy sitting on the potty to looking at the stars that he had earned by staying dry since her last visit. An analysis of the antecedents or triggers as well as of the consequences was necessary to explain what had been happening.

The programme described by Azrin and Foxx in their book *Toilet training in less than a day*, is a fun way to help toilet train a child that uses all of the behavioural principles in the examples above, and the strategies for teaching new behaviour (see Chapter 7). Their programme starts with modelling by a doll that pees and then is based on prompting and reinforcing the behaviour that is wanted, this includes a lot of reinforcement for being dry and practicing with frequent checks for dry pants. Whilst they used sweets as reinforcers, along with praise, cuddles and involving other significant adults, sweets are not something that is recommended and the programme works as well with other reinforcers such as special stickers. A mum that had used *Toilet training in less than a day* with her own four children and recently bought it for one of them to use with one of their children posted the following review on Amazon:

To be honest, I bought this book way back in the 70s and used it to potty train my four children. Of course it doesn't work in less than a day (neither do Father Christmas nor the Tooth fairy exist, you know), but I found it a brilliant way to get the children started and compared to other mums my kids were potty trained relatively quickly.

The reason why I am writing this review is that I was looking for something to help my own daughters potty train their kids – and was delighted to find the book is still in print – no mean feat after more than 40 years!

These examples show the importance of clearly defining the target behaviour and all of the steps to achieve it and also of identifying both possible reinforcers and achievable goals leading to effective interventions to support our children's learning.

Further reading

Azrin, N. and Foxx, R. (1997) Toilet training in less than a day. London, Pan Books

An eating problem

A behaviour that a child engages in often is, by definition, reinforcing, and one way of increasing a behaviour that does not occur very often is to link it to the reinforcing behaviour. This is often referred to as "When …then". For example, Johnny loved watching TV but would not do homework and hated showing work to his parents. When Johnny had to earn his TV viewing by doing half an hour's homework and showing it to his parents, he soon learned to do the homework willingly and subsequently, although this can take time, as a result of parental praise, to enjoy it. Homework can be a cause of stress and arguments between parents and children so it was also important that, initially, his parents praised Johnny's *effort* rather than commenting on the quality. In time this also led to other rewards, like better marks and positive teacher attention. So, arranging for activities that children like to do as a reward for doing those they find hard can be helpful and, in the end, lead to longer term rewards like enjoyment of studying that were established by immediate rewards.

Current rates of childhood obesity are concerning, with 26% of five-year-old children in Wales, and 22% in England, overweight and over 11.5% obese, with the majority of obese children (82.5%) remaining obese four years later. Not surprisingly therefore, given the health problems related to obesity, ensuring that children eat a healthy diet is a concern for many parents. Children whose diets have plenty of fruit and vegetables are less likely to become obese than children on poorer diets and, in the longer term, eating plenty of fruit and vegetables protects against many cancers, lowers the risk of coronary heart disease and helps prevent diabetes. However, teaching children to eat a healthy diet can be a challenge for parents and a child saying that they don't like something, particularly refusing certain foods, is a common problem. The key to changing children's food preferences is repeated tasting, children come to like fruit and vegetables because the taste buds learn to recognise and accept new tastes.

The school based Food Dudes Healthy Eating Programme, developed at Bangor University, has demonstrated the effectiveness of using the behavioural principles of role-modelling, rewards and repeated tastings in getting children to taste new foods and increasing their regular consumption of fruit and vegetables. The fun programme targets children and, indirectly, their families. Children watch the DVD adventures of the 'Food Dudes', a group of children who are fun, cool, slightly older than themselves and very successful. By eating fruit and vegetables, the Dudes equip themselves with the superpowers they need to vanquish General Junk and his Junk Punks, who are taking away the energy of the world by depriving it of healthy food. Through words and catchy songs, children are encouraged to taste fruit and vegetables and earn Food Dudes rewards, pencil cases, pencils, juggling balls and other small rewards.

In the Food Dudes programme, children develop pride in seeing themselves as fruit and vegetable eaters with the greatest gains shown by children who ate the least fruit and vegetables at the start and who need them most. The programme effects extended beyond the school context into the home environment and were long lasting.

Whilst not every child has access to the Food Dudes programme, the principles are relevant to helping parents to solve problems of children's fussy eating, particularly the idea of making eating healthy food fun. Lucy was six-years-old. Her parents were concerned that she ate so few foods. They had tried a variety of approaches suggested by friends and relatives, from what they called bribery to confrontation and punishment, but the problem remained. Lucy's parents kept records about what she ate and about mealtimes in general and once they had a clear picture of the problem, it was obvious that meal times had become an unpleasant and anxiety provoking time for them all. It was also clear that there was not a lot of role modelling of meal-time behaviour for Lucy as the family did not often eat together.

The first step in the plan was to arrange for her parents to eat with Lucy and to let Lucy have the foods she liked. The initial goal was to make meal times fun in other ways. Her parents talked with her about things unrelated to food, what they had been doing during the day or what they might do after the meal was over for example, and they gave Lucy attention for appropriate behaviour, such as coming to the table when asked, using a knife and fork, etc. After a couple of weeks, when the initial goal of making mealtimes a pleasant joint family activity was reached, they moved on.

Lucy was offered food that her parents were eating and whenever she refused a particular food, her parents were encouraged to say: "You haven't learned to like this yet but you probably will when you are a bit older". Introducing the idea that we learn to like foods and that getting used to new foods is a learning process is really helpful to children. Next they started to put very small quantities of foods Lucy did not like onto her plate – two or three peas. They explained to Lucy that she did not have to eat it but that if she did she would be rewarded by having a choice of pudding or ice cream. At first she ignored the peas and her parents said nothing but after a couple of days she pushed them into the mashed potato and ate them. They immediately gave her lots of praise and attention for eating the peas and the choice of a pudding. They repeated giving her peas for several days before introducing another food that she had previously rejected. This time it was very small florets of broccoli. Throughout this process she was praised for trying new and healthy foods that she had previously rejected. Her parents reminded her that learning to eat new foods was not easy but was part of growing up and explained why certain foods were important for her health.

Another way that her parents helped Lucy was to let her prepare and help cook the food. This gave her another reason for wanting to try it, to taste the results of her own efforts. With these gradual changes in the way that Lucy's parents approached her eating problems, that took place over several months, they helped her to eat and enjoy many foods that she had previously rejected. They had also learned some basic rules about teaching new behaviour and coping with problem behaviour. These are:

1. Make learning fun.
2. Model the behaviour that you want.
3. Set small achievable goals for children in order to make it easy for them to succeed.
4. Offer the same food once the child has tried it to ensure repeat tastings before moving on to new foods.
5. Arrange small rewards, and ensure that they are accompanied by parental praise and attention.
6. Predict success by reminding the child that it is a learning process and is part of growing up: "you haven't learned to like broccoli yet but you will do".

These ideas enabled Lucy's parents to help Lucy to learn to eat a range of different foods and to become better at teaching other new behaviours to her. They now knew how to focus on ways of helping her to learn rather than on provoking confrontation about activities they had failed to teach her.

Another family used a different strategy. Simon was a fussy eater and his parents put a lot of food on Simon's plate in the hope that he would eat some of it. But he played with it, ate a little of the things he liked and never had the experience of a clean plate. They decided to give Simon mini-meals, initially only with foods that he was already eating, this meant very small amounts of each item, for example, a third of a fish finger, a dessertspoonful of mashed potato and a small spoonful of baked beans. When he had a clean plate, Simon was praised for having a clean plate and was given the choice of more of the same food or he could have a pudding, generally an ice-cream. Like Lucy, the praise that Simon received made mealtimes a lot more pleasant. Simon responded immediately and his plate was clean from the start. Initially he immediately opted for the pudding but over time started to ask for more of his first course before asking for pudding. Simon's parents left this plan in place for two weeks before moving on and starting to add very small amounts of other food to Simon's plate. In the meantime, they told Simon that they could remember times when they had not liked food but had now learned to do so, telling him that some things, olives for example, were tastes that they had only learned to enjoy as adults. They also told him that learning to like foods takes time. This plan worked well and within a couple of months Simon had significantly extended the range of foods that he would eat.

A key feature in the success of these programmes was that the parents recognised that what they wanted to achieve was a long-term goal and that enabled them to stay calm and make mealtimes a pleasant time. So, using key strategies from the Food Dudes programme, role modelling, rewarding and repeated tasting enabled these parents to support their children in learning to make and enjoy healthy food choices.

Avoidance and anxiety-based problems

Some behaviours are reinforced by the removal of negative consequences. As we have seen this can often be the case when giving the child what they are demanding, or abandoning trying to get the child to do something, stops the child from crying, having a tantrum or demanding. But the same applies also to children.

Antecedent	Behaviour	Consequences
Mum finds coat lying on the floor. Mum tells Joanne o. How many times have I told you Mum begins to shout and threatens to stop Joanne from going out.	No response from Joanne who is texting her friend Joanne hangs up the coat reluctantly.	Mum becomes angry. Mum stops shouting but says why didnt you do it the first time. Joanne returns to texting.

In this example, like the morning example with Steven, Joanne's behaviour was eventually reinforced by the removal of an aversive situation, Mum's nagging and threat of punishment. Unfortunately, when children finally respond in these situations they are unlikely to get praise because the parent is still feeling angry. However, this is a poor way of teaching children to do something, it only teaches them to hang the coat up when Mum's reminders become irritating. They hang it up in order to stop the nagging. So, the reinforcer for the child is the removal of an unpleasant event, nagging. It does not teach the child to hang up their coat when they come through the door. This requires a different strategy. This distinction is important since it explains why we should always teach and reward appropriate behaviour, because, when behaviour is rewarded with praise, the reward can eventually be faded out and the behaviour, cleaning teeth for example, will be maintained because it feels more comfortable to do it.

A different sort of problem occurs when what is being experienced are negative sensations in our own bodies. This is the case with anxiety-based problems in which, rather than doing something to avoid or remove nagging, our uncomfortable feelings are cues to avoid the stressful situation all together. If we respond to the anxiety produced by avoidance, this can become a pattern which, in cases of extreme avoidance, we call a phobia.

As humans we have two responses to perceived danger or distress, one is to fight or challenge the danger and the other is to run away. When we find ourselves in a situation of danger we experience a series of physical bodily changes, our blood pressure rises, we become tense, we may start to shake or feel hot and to breathe more rapidly and our body releases adrenalin. This prepares us for the fight or flight response. Depending on the nature of the perceived threat and how we interpret it we then respond. Avoidance is triggered by the flight response and removes us from the anxiety-provoking event. It is reinforced because we become calm in a different place where the perceived threat is no longer present.

Many people dislike things like spiders and mice but this only occasionally leads to extreme avoidance. The avoidance behaviour is reinforced because we see a rapid movement, a mouse that triggers arousal and our flight response, so we run away. Our behaviour is reinforced by a change in how we feel because we become calm and feel OK again in a situation away from the perceived threat. This makes it likely that we will do it again and also likely that we will avoid the situation where we had this negative experience.

Post-traumatic stress is an anxiety-based condition where people, as a result of a bad experience, become overwhelmed by fear and can have repeated flashbacks to the situation that make it impossible for them to continue to live normally. Examples of situations that can produce post-traumatic stress can include seeing someone get injured or killed, being injured themselves or being the subject of domestic abuse or rape. It is particularly common following experience of war-time or following natural disasters. News coverage of anxiety-provoking situations such as wars, road traffic accidents, abuse and stories of murders, burglaries etc. can act as triggers and add to people's anxieties.

Sometimes, an avoidance response arises from a one-trial learning experience and sometimes it is repeated exposure to a lower level threat. An example of a one-off experience happened to a child, who as a toddler was stung by a wasp that he tried to pick up, and this generalised to a fear of any flying insects. At other times avoidance can develop as a result of lower but repeated exposure to a stress-producing situation. So a child who is teased at school might, over time, develop a dislike of school that becomes a phobia with even the thought of being at school triggering an anxiety response that is only calmed by refusing to go to school.

Some avoidance behaviours are conditioned by seeing other people behave in particular ways. One mother reported having seen her own mother scream and jump onto a chair at the sight of a mouse for example. This example of the modelling principle left her with a manageable, but uncomfortable, feeling in their presence.

It is important to consider whether the anxiety arises from a lack of skills to deal with the situation. Some children are easily aroused and seem programmed to have an anxiety response more quickly than others. In the case of children on the autistic spectrum, many situations can provoke anxiety, such as transitions from one activity to another, or having to manage social situations. It is important to consider ways of making the world very predictable for these children and the strategies that have been developed to treat phobias or anxiety are also helpful in supporting them.

Many social phobias arise because the individual has not got the skills to deal with the situation. This may be being bullied, called names or teased at school or not being able to do the expected schoolwork. These problems require a strategy to manage the situation as well as teaching the child to manage their emotional responses. If the problem arises because the child cannot do what is expected or required in school, they need an individualised learning plan. If they are being bullied they need to be taught strategies for getting help. In addition to teaching the child to manage their anxiety, the demands of the situation need to be achievable for the child.

In the case of bullying it is important to work with other children to ensure that they learn to support the child that is being bullied. Most children say that bullying is wrong but many do not know what to do to stop it and research shows that the long term effects of being bullied are significant. Furthermore, adults who were victimised say that it was not so much the behaviour of the bully that they remember but the fact that no one did anything about it. A very effective school-based programme called KiVa was developed in Finland to help reduce bullying. KiVa is a whole school approach which, whilst directly supporting the victimised child, focuses on the behaviour of bystanders by giving them skills and strategies to support the victims of bullying. KiVa is now being introduced into schools in the UK and is also demonstrating similarly good results. The KiVa website has a useful booklet for parents on how to handle bullying (www.kivaprogram.net).

A child on the autistic spectrum who needs extra transition time to cope with a change of activity may need extra scaffolding, both at home and at school. At school letting them be the child that rings the bell in the classroom to let others know that a transition to another activity is coming up can help as it gives them this extra bit of transition time warning. Other strategies include giving them personal picture timetables or ensuring that they do not spend too long in a situation that is stressful for them, such as circle time or other social activities, and arranging that a brief stay will be rewarded with an activity that they like, often a solitary play activity.

Once we understand the triggers for anxiety-based responses we can start to help children to deal with them. In fact the release of adrenalin is quite short term, allowing for bodily preparation to run away or to stand and fight. If a person with a flight response can be persuaded to remain in the presence of an anxiety-promoting object, such as a mouse or spider, their anxiety will reduce fairly quickly and they will learn that the feared object is not a threat. Persuading people to stay in the presence of feared objects is not easy however a number of well tried and tested strategies have been developed to address phobias.

Training in relaxation skills helps the body to counteract the negative physiological effects of anxiety. There are a number of programmes and resources for children but one of the best researched is the Coping Cat programme developed by Kendall that includes workbooks and a CD rom (www.workbookpublishing.com). When this approach is paired with gradual exposure to the feared situation this is called desensitisation. Relaxation means learning to monitor bodily sensations and do things to counteract them, such as controlling breathing by practising taking deep breaths, doing activities to relax the body through self-talk and through focusing on tensing and relaxing muscles. It is particularly useful to initially train these skills at a time when the person is not feeling anxious.

Teaching stress-reducing self-talk that challenges the negative thoughts that are associated with the anxiety has been shown to be helpful. Teaching children to say "I can stay calm, I can calm myself" or "This situation is difficult but it is possible to manage" or "I can take some deep breaths", gives them self-instructions about how to handle the situation and also serve as a distraction.

Desensitisation of a fear of mice

A grandmother whose fear of mice had resulted in her becoming almost house-bound sought help with this problem. The successful programme involved:

1. Teaching relaxation, including monitoring to identify how her body was feeling, tensing and relaxing muscles and practising breathing skills. (There are lots of audio aids to teaching relaxing).
2. Learning positive self-talk about the fact that she was seeking help, that her problem was not unusual (*normalising*) and that she was doing something

about it. It also included reminding herself about the things she would be able to do once she overcame this fear and this included visiting her children and grandchildren.

3. Visualising a mouse and to then use her relaxation skills to self-calm whilst holding on to the image of the mouse.

4. The next step involved exposure to pictures and video footage of mice, again paired with relaxation and positive self-talk until she was able to look at the pictures and stay calm.

5. The next step involved exposure to mice in cages in a pet shop and again practising all of the earlier steps in managing her anxiety and remaining calm.

6. She then watched another person handling a live mouse.

Of course it is difficult to arrange real life exposure to mice but, following these steps, she felt sufficiently confident that she had the skills to remain calm if she did see one, probably a fairly unlikely event as she certainly did not have any in her home, and was able to resume normal life.

Relaxation skills and positive self-talk form part of the desensitisation and gradual exposure strategy, regardless of whether the problem seems logical or not. Fear of mice might seem less logical than fear of being bullied or ridiculed in public but the bodily sensations and effects in terms of avoidance are the same. In the bullying situation, learning alternative more assertive responses can be very effective but these skills need to be rehearsed after having first practised managing anxiety through relaxation and self-talk.

Many parents report that children are afraid of the dark but if their parents allow them to sleep with the light on they are not exposed to the feared situation and can, therefore, never learn that it is safe. This is a problem that is important to address since there are now plenty of studies that demonstrate that quality sleep is compromised by sleeping with a light on, as this has a significant effect in depressing the production of melatonin that regulates sleep cycles. Other studies demonstrate the importance of at least nine hours of good sleep for children and even more when they are younger. These are good reasons for a desensitisation programme that could involve a dimmer switch, allowing for the level of light to be gradually lowered, or a timer that puts the light off after a while or sitting in the dark with a parent present and being rewarded for learning to stay in the dark.

Help for children's anxiety-based problems involves first talking with confidence with the child about the fact that anxiety is a normal bodily response and that solutions are possible, then using the following steps:

1. Identify very clearly exactly what the situation is where the anxiety response occurs.
2. Help the child to identify their bodily cues that they are becoming anxious.

3. Teach relaxation skills, body monitoring and breathing.
4. Identify clearly the goal that the child is working on.
5. Prompt positive self-talk about the problem.
6. Introduce the problem situation in imagination and again practise the relaxation and self-talk.
7. Identify and talk with the child about other ways to behave in the situation. Identify what alternative skills or strategies need to be taught in order to handle the situation.
8. Role play/rehearse alternative coping strategies.
9. Set up a reward programme to encourage the child to work towards a solution and reward small steps.
10. Where appropriate work with others in the situation to support the child, for example by offering support to the victims of bullying.

Careful attention to anxiety-provoking situations and the patterns of avoidance that arise from it will enable us to ensure that the demands placed on children are realistic, that the environment is encouraged to support them and that they are given help to develop the skills to handle difficult situations and overcome anxieties.

References for the evidence cited in the intervention examples in this chapter can be found in the *Practitioner Guide to Enhancing Parenting Skills* (Hutchings and Williams, 2019) along with references to other sources of information that have contributed to the ideas in this book.

Useful further reading sources:

Toxic Childhood: How The Modern World Is Damaging Our Children and What We Can Do About It

Sue Palmer (2007)

(ISBN 13: 9780752880914)

Incredible Years: A Troubleshooting Guide for Parents of Children Aged 2 to 8

Carolyn Webster-Stratton

(ISBN 13: 9781895642025)

Parenting the Strong-Willed Child: The Clinically Proven Five-Week Program for Parents of Two-Six Year Olds, Third Edition

Rex Forehand and Nicholas Long

(ISBN 13: 9780071383011)